"Every page of this useful and engaging guide is informed by 9to5's years of experience confronting the problems of working women. Knowledgeable, accessible, incisive, this book provides solid information and creative solutions, both legal and nonlegal. With this, 9to5 makes one more solid contribution to victimized women and their advocates, hence to the possibilities for equality."

—Catharine A. MacKinnon
Professor of Law
University of Michigan

"For 20 years, 9to5 has given practical advice and strong support to employers and employees alike. No one has tracked sexual harassment more closely than 9to5, and this one-of-a-kind book is a much-needed guide to help deal with an ugly workplace problem of the 1990s."

—Carol Kleiman
Chicago Tribune, **nationally syndicated columnist and**
author of *The 100 Best Jobs in the 1990s & Beyond*

"A very thoughtful and practical guide to combating a serious problem that is not very well understood by many, perhaps most, men."

—Ray Marshall
Former Secretary of Labor

"Everything you wanted to know about sexual harassment, but were either too embarrassed to ask, or didn't know who to ask . . . very useful to both victims of sexual harassment and businesses who want to safeguard against it."

—Margaret M. Crawford
Director, Human Resources
Harley-Davidson, Inc.

D0660848

"An essential guide for every union steward and activist. It's got everything—vital information on laws and strategies with a whole chapter devoted to the role of unions combating sexual harassment, including contract language. Unions have a special role to play. 9to5's guide helps us to do that. No union should be without it."

—Joyce Miller
CLUW (Coalition of Labor Union Women)

"This new 9to5 guide cuts through the tangle of conflicting attitudes, opinions and presumptions about sexual harassment, an issue made even knottier by the Thomas-Hill hearings and other high-profile skirmishes in our ongoing gender wars. Bravo and Cassedy present a clear and definitive picture of what constitutes sexual harassment, why it occurs and what should be done about it."

—Nina J. Easton
Staff Writer
Los Angeles Times Magazine

"Sexual harassment festers in every kind of workplace, in every sector of our economy. The groundbreaking work of 9to5 will make it easier to fight back and win."

—John J. Sweeney
President, *Service Employees International Union,*
AFL-CIO

"This book is great! It gives folks a tool to fight back with. It's a book no working woman should be without."

—Jim Hightower
Populists spokesperson, former Texas Commissioner
of Agriculture

The 9to5 Guide to Combating Sexual Harassment

Candid Advice from 9to5, The National
Association of Working Women

Ellen Bravo
Ellen Cassedy

John Wiley & Sons, Inc.
New York • Chichester • Brisbane • Toronto • Singapore

This publication is designed to provide accurate and authoritative information in regard to the subject matter covered. It is sold with the understanding that the publisher is not engaged in rendering legal, accounting, or other professional service. If legal advice or other expert assistance is required, the services of a competent professional person should be sought. *From a Declaration of Principles jointly adopted by a Committee of the American Bar Association and a Committee of Publishers.*

Library of Congress Cataloging-in-Publication Data

Bravo, Ellen.
    The 9 to 5 guide to combating sexual harassment candid advice from 9 to 5, the National Association of Working Women / Ellen Bravo, Ellen Cassedy.
       p.   cm.
    ISBN 0-471-57576-3 (alk. paper)
    1. Sexual harassment of women—United States. I. Cassedy, Ellen. II. 9 to 5, National Association of Working Women (U.S.) III. Title.   IV. Title: Nine to five guide to combating sexual harassment.
HD6060.5.U5B73   1992   92-9793
331.4'133—dc20

10 9 8 7 6 5 4 3 2
Printed and bound by Courier Companies, Inc.

Acknowledgments

Above all, we are grateful to the many women who shared their experiences with us. Their stories appear throughout the book and helped shape the advice presented here.

We would also like to thank the following individuals for their assistance: Margo Anderson, Alice Ballard, Ramona Cerda Schwan, Margaret Crawford, Diana Finch, Heather Hauck, Sharon Hoahing, Dottie Jones, Michelle Keys, Sharon Kinsella, Joyce Kornbluh, Nancy Lessin, Theodore M. Lieverman, Ruth Needleman, Karen Nussbaum, Barbara Otto, Anna Padia, Lois Roberts, Roger Scholl, Debby Seagraves, Jean Sherwenka, Kim Wade, Alexandra White, Faith Wohl, Victoria Yocum, and Barbara Zack Quindel.

We're especially grateful to our families—Larry, Nat, and Craig, and Jeff, Tim, and Meg—for their encouragement and support.

Contents

Introduction

A project manager went to her boss's office to pick up her paycheck. "Come and get it," he crooned and pointed to the envelope he'd tucked into the fly of his trousers.

A supervisor observed a group of male workers laughing over a postcard depicting a nude woman having sex with a goat. Later he saw one of the men slip the postcard into the locker of a new female hire. The supervisor didn't know what to do. "If I make an issue of it," he said, "I'm afraid either her neck is going to be on the line or mine is."

A group of graphic artists couldn't believe their ears one evening. A coworker had turned up the volume on his tape player and was broadcasting the gang rape scene from a pornographic movie.

The project manager, the supervisor, and the graphic artists are some of the more than 100,000 employees and employers who have telephoned the toll-free 9to5 Job Problem Hotline since it was established in 1989. (The number of the hotline is printed at the end of this book.) Among those reporting problems and receiving advice have been beauticians, supervisors, sales representatives, medical assistants, factory workers, teachers, cashiers, waitresses, library workers, computer operators, executive secretaries, therapists, bartenders, bakers, and zookeepers—as well as one symphony-orchestra manager, one oil-rig supervisor, and one topless dancer.

They call about unequal pay and unsafe computer equipment, pensions and maternity leave, who serves the coffee, and how to get promoted. Some tell of being asked to perform bizarre tasks—to sharpen 1,400 pencils, one right after the other; or to snip the boss's nose hairs, to clean his dentures, or to carry his urine specimen, still warm, to the lab.

And some call about sexual harassment. Ever since 9to5 was founded in 1973 to give voice to working women's concerns, unwelcome sexual attention at the workplace has been viewed within the organization as a significant and disturbing issue.

HARASSMENT GOES PUBLIC

When 9to5 began, the problem of unwanted sexual attention at work had no name and little visibility. Neither corporate nor government leaders were expected to worry about what some men were doing to annoy some hapless (and, in their eyes, probably provocative) women. The issue was seen as a trivial matter involving nothing more than individual personality conflicts and office etiquette. The term *sexual harassment* didn't yet exist—the courts were years away from recognizing the concept.

But the two decades that followed saw big changes. Millions of women entered the workplace and stayed—because they had to. (A full 58 percent of women workers are single, divorced, widowed, separated, or married to men who earn less than $15,000.) Once women were firmly established in the labor force in large and growing numbers, the problem of sexual harassment began to come out of the closet.

The term itself was popularized in such books as Lin Farley's *Sexual Shakedown: The Sexual Harassment of Women on the Job* (McGraw-Hill, 1978) and Catherine A. MacKinnon's *Sexual Harassment of Working Women: A Case of Sex Discrimination* (Yale University Press, 1979). Pressure grew for a solution. Speakouts and public hearings were held. Women's magazines and other media sources publicized the issue. Lawsuits moved through the courts. The government, academia, and some corporate leaders began to take the problem seriously. Still, in most workplaces and across the nation as a whole, the issue remained nearly invisible— until October of 1991. Public awareness of sexual harassment then took a giant step forward.

THE CLARENCE THOMAS HEARINGS:
DID HE OR DIDN'T HE?

In October 1991, the Senate Judiciary Committee completed hearings to consider President Bush's nomination of conservative Appellate Judge Clarence Thomas to the Supreme Court. The nomination appeared headed for easy approval on the Senate floor. Then, two days before the scheduled vote, a startling challenge to Thomas's character arose. A radio reporter learned that the FBI had interviewed a former government lawyer, Anita Hill. She told investigators that, a decade earlier, when Thomas was her boss, he had repeatedly subjected her to unwelcome sexual attention. He'd insisted on discussing sex and pornographic movies, Hill said, and pressured her for dates.

Informed by the FBI of Hill's allegations, the Senate Judiciary Committee had decided not to pursue them. But once the story hit the media, a public outcry led the committee to reconvene. Throughout the Columbus Day weekend, millions of Americans spent hours in front of the television watching committee members contend with the graphic and gruesome details of sexual harassment.

Thomas steadfastly denied Hill's allegations, the Senate approved his nomination, and he was appointed Associate Justice of the Supreme Court. But the storm stirred up by Hill's charges wasn't over. Throughout the country, sexual harassment became a matter of heated discussion. Countless women were moved to discuss their own harassment experiences publicly—often for the first time. Thousands called the 9to5 Job Problem Hotline. In trembling whispers or in voices boiling with anger, some recounted incidents that had occurred years or even decades earlier, while others asked what to do about the harasser sitting at the next desk. Employers also called for advice about implementing antiharassment policies.

Some callers said they'd learned only through the Thomas hearings that sexual harassment was illegal. Many were outraged by the Senate's unsympathetic treatment of Anita Hill and wanted to know how to complain to their Congressional representatives. They felt that if more senators had been women (only two were), Thomas would never have been confirmed.

Some callers believed that the Thomas hearings sent a strong and discouraging message to harassment victims—when it's her word against his, he wins. But others felt that by bringing the issue into the public eye, the hearings had a positive impact. Sexual harassment ". . . is one of the nation's dirty little secrets," Donna E. Shalala, chancellor of the University of Wisconsin, told the *Boston Globe* (10/16/91), "and it had to be brought out." As Anita Hill herself said after the hearings, "The silence has been broken."

A PERVASIVE PROBLEM

As a result of the hearings, even those who weren't sure what to think about Anita Hill and Clarence Thomas learned that sexual harassment is a pervasive problem. It happens to women in every profession from waitress to corporate executive. It occurs at every level of the corporate hierarchy and in every kind of business and industry. It's carried out by superiors and subordinates, coworkers and clients. Some men are also sexually harassed, though on a far smaller scale. (To avoid cumbersome language, the victim is often referred to here as "she" and the harasser and employer as "he.")

- In a survey of federal employees conducted by the U.S. Merit Protection Services Board in 1980, 42 percent of females and 15 percent of males said they'd been harassed on the job. A follow-up survey in 1987 yielded nearly identical results.
- Since 1980, more than 38,500 charges of sexual harassment have been filed with the federal government.
- In a 1990 study of 20,000 military employees conducted by the Department of Defense, 64 percent of the females and 17 percent of the males said they'd been harassed.
- In numerous corporate studies carried out by management consultant Freada Klein, at least 15 percent of women employees said they'd been harassed within the past 12 months.
- In a 1987 study, 37 percent of women at the Department of Labor said they'd been sexually harassed on the job.
- In a 1989 study, the National Law Journal found that of 3,000 women lawyers at 250 top law firms, 60 percent had been harassed at some point in their careers.
- A survey of United Nations employees showed 50 percent of women and 31 percent of men had experienced or witnessed harassment by higher-ups.
- Nearly half of the 832 working women in researcher Barbara

Gutek's 1985 study said they'd been harassed. None had taken any legal action. Only 22 percent had ever told anybody about the harassment.

- In a 1988 survey of Fortune 500 companies conducted by *Working Woman* magazine, almost 90 percent of the respondents reported receiving complaints of harassment. More than a third had been sued.

- In a poll released in 1991 by the National Association for Female Executives, 53 percent of 1,300 respondents had either been harassed themselves or knew someone who had.

- More than half of the professional women surveyed in 1990 by *Working Smart*, a business newsletter, said they'd been harassed.

- In a 1986 study by the Association of American Colleges, 32 percent of tenured faculty women and 49 percent of untenured women at Harvard University had experienced harassment.

- So have 40 percent of undergraduate women students and 28 percent of female graduate students, according to consultant Freada Klein.

- In a survey conducted at the time of the Thomas hearings, *Newsweek* (10/21/91) found that 21 percent of women polled said they'd been harassed.

- At the same time, the *New York Times* (10/11/91) found that four out of ten women polled had been harassed and that five out of ten men reported they'd said or done something that could be construed as harassment.

SEXUAL HARASSMENT IN CONTEXT

Sexual harassment doesn't take place in a vacuum. It is the relatively low status of women in the work world that makes the problem so widespread and so persistent. And if harassment stems from women's inferior position on the job, it also functions to *keep* women there.

Despite laws against discrimination, Census Bureau figures show that women bring home less than two-thirds of the pay men receive. Women college graduates earn about the same salary as men who hold only a high school diploma. Furthermore, the Bureau of Labor Statistics reports that the segregation of women into lower-paying jobs is not a thing of the past—in some cases it's even getting worse. Fewer than 3 percent of the top jobs at Fortune 500 companies are held by women, according to a 1991 study by the Feminist Majority Foundation. When 9to5 began, it was difficult to get people to recognize these facts. The idea that women weren't being treated equally in the work world and that they *deserved* equality was far from commonly accepted. Today, most people agree that working women don't receive equal treatment in the workplace—and that they should.

UNRESOLVED DEBATE

The debate over sexual harassment, on the other hand, is nowhere near being resolved. People don't agree on what harassment is, how serious it is, and what steps should be taken to stop it.

Should the term *harassment* apply only to unwelcome *physical* advances? Or should it encompass other offensive statements and actions? Who defines *offensive*? Do women really mind the attention? If a man puts his arm around a woman at work or tells an off-color joke, should he be hauled into court? Should women learn to speak out against harassment or simply to live with it? How can a manager ban harassment without stifling all friendly banter on the job? What, if anything, should be done about the pinups in the men's room?

Sexual harassment is relatively simple to define—it is repeated, unwanted sexual attention on the job. In most cases, it's easy to tell when it's happening. Often, whether a particular kind of behavior is offensive or not depends on who's doing it, to whom, how often, with what tone of voice and facial expression, and on how the behavior is received.

Sexual harassment can be stopped. The majority of men are not harassers. Of those who are, most will stop once harassment becomes less acceptable and the consequences more severe. Many managers want a work environment that treats all employees with equal respect and an atmosphere free of harassment. But more companies need to promote these goals with clearly stated policies, and the laws must be strengthened. These are not simple goals—but they're not unattainable, either.

This book is for anyone who has ever been sexually harassed. It is for managers and corporate leaders in search of practical solutions. It is for anyone trying to figure out what is offensive and what isn't. It's for students, faculty, and university employees, for union members and leaders, for blue-, pink-, and white-collar workers. It's for the friends and families of harassment victims. It's for attorneys who want to understand the effects of harassment on victim and employer alike. It's for anyone who wants to put a stop to harassment.

We hope this book will enable those being harassed to take action against the abuse, obtain support from others, help institute a strong workplace policy, and file a formal complaint, if necessary. We aim to help managers and union leaders prevent harassment and deal with it effectively if it does occur.

The book draws on our work with employers and employees across the country, those individuals who have called the hotline, become involved in our local chapters, and participated in antiharassment training. In these pages, we lay out the latest thinking about what constitutes harassment; outline the laws, their history, and how to use them; describe the effects of harassment; answer critics who question the importance of the issue; and make recommendations for the future. The book contains exercises and model policies used in the seminars we have conducted at a variety of workplaces.

WHAT 9TO5 IS

The organization known as 9to5 began in 1973 when a group of ten women workers gathered after a Boston seminar and began to trade stories. The group grew into a nationwide effort that garnered the attention of management and the trade-union movement—and even Hollywood. (In 1980, the movie *Nine to Five* was a box office hit, reflecting many of the concerns raised by the organization.) In 1981, 9to5 helped create a sister organization, District 925 of the Service Employees International Union, for those employees interested in being in a union. (SEIU, the fourth largest and fastest growing union in the United States, represents a wide variety of workers, from janitors to doctors and lawyers.)

Over the years, 9to5 has been in contact with thousands of women who encountered sexual harassment on their jobs. With great courage and much hard work, they have started support groups, told painful stories to policymakers, and organized for change. This guide is dedicated to them.

1

What Sexual Harassment Is— and Is Not

Louette Colombano was one of the first female police officers in her San Francisco district. While listening to the watch commander, she and the other officers stood at attention with their hands behind their backs. The officer behind her unzipped his fly and rubbed his penis against her hands.

Diane, a buyer, was preparing to meet an out-of-town client for dinner when she received a message: her boss had informed the client that she would spend the night with him. Diane sent word that she couldn't make it to dinner. The next day she was fired.

Few people would disagree that these are clear-cut examples of sexual harassment. Touching someone in a deliberately sexual way, demanding that an employee engage in sex or lose her job— such behavior is clearly out of bounds. (It's also *illegal*, as will be discussed in Chapter 3.) But in less obvious cases, many people are confused about where to draw the line.

IS IT HARASSMENT?

Is all sexual conversation inappropriate at work? Is every kind of touching off limits? Consider the following examples. In your opinion, which, if any, constitute sexual harassment?

- A male manager asks a female subordinate to lunch to discuss a new project.
- A man puts his arm around a woman at work.
- A woman tells an off-color joke.
- These comments are made at the workplace:

   "Your hair looks terrific."

   "That outfit's a knockout."

   "Did you get any last night?"

The answer in each of these cases is, "It depends." Each one *could* be an example of sexual harassment—or it could be acceptable behavior.

Take the case of the manager asking a female subordinate to lunch to discuss a new project. Suppose this manager often has such lunchtime meetings with his employees, male and female. Everyone is aware that he likes to get out of the office environment in order to get to know the associates a little better and to learn how they function—for example, whether they prefer frequent meetings or written reports, detailed instructions or more delegation of responsibility. The female subordinate in this case may feel she's being treated just like other colleagues and be glad to receive the individual attention.

On the other hand, suppose this subordinate has been trying for some time, unsuccessfully, to be assigned to an interesting project. The only woman who does get plum assignments spends a lot of time out of the office with the boss; the two of them are rumored to be sleeping together. The lunch may represent an opportunity to move ahead, but it could mean that the manager expects a physical relationship in return. In this case, an invitation to lunch with the boss is laden with unwelcome sexual overtones.

An arm around the shoulder, an off-color joke, comments about someone's appearance, or even sexual remarks may or may not be offensive. What matters is the relationship between the two parties and how each of them feels.

"Your hair looks terrific," for instance, could be an innocuous compliment if it were tossed off by one coworker to another as they passed in the hall. But imagine this same phrase coming from a male boss bending down next to his secretary's ear and speaking in a suggestive whisper. Suddenly, these innocent-sounding words take on a different meaning. The body language and tone of voice signify something sexual. While the comment itself may not amount to much, the secretary is left to wonder *what else the boss has in mind.*

On the other hand, even words that may seem grossly inappropriate—"Did you get any last night?"—can be harmless in certain work situations. One group of male and female assembly-line workers talked like this all the time. What made it okay? They were friends and equals—no one in the group had power over any of the others. They were all comfortable with the banter. They hadn't drawn up a list specifying which words were acceptable to the group and which were not. But they had worked together for some time and knew one another well. Their remarks were made with affection and accepted as good-natured. No one intended to offend—and no one was offended. The assembly-line area was relatively isolated, so the workers weren't in danger of bothering anyone outside their group. Had a new person joined the group who wasn't comfortable with this kind of talk, the others would have stopped it. They might have thought the new person uptight, they might not have liked the new atmosphere, but they would have respected and honored any request to eliminate the remarks.

This is the essence of combating sexual harassment—creating a workplace that is built on mutual respect.

LOOKING AT HARASSMENT

Try assessing whether each of the following scenarios constitutes sexual harassment. Then consider the analysis that follows.

Scenario 1

Justine works in a predominantly male department. She has tried to fit in, even laughing on occasion at the frequent sexual jokes. The truth is, though, that she gets more irritated by the jokes each day. It is well known in the department that Justine has an out-of-town boyfriend whom she sees most weekends. Nonetheless, Franklin, one of Justine's coworkers, has said he has the "hots" for her and that—boyfriend or not—he's willing to do almost anything to get a date with her. One day, Sarah, another of Justine's coworkers, overheard their boss talking to Franklin in the hallway. "If you can get her to go to bed with you," the boss said, "I'll take you out to dinner. Good luck." They chuckled and went their separate ways. (From the consulting firm of Jane C. Edmonds & Associates, Inc., *Boston Globe*, 10/24/91.)

The boss is out of line. True, he probably didn't intend anyone to overhear him. But why was he having this conversation in the hallway? What was he doing having the conversation at all? The boss is responsible for keeping the workplace free of harassment. Instead, he's giving Franklin an incentive to make sexual advances to a coworker and then to brag about it.

The conversation may constitute harassment not only of Justine but also of Sarah, who overheard the conversation. A reasonable woman might easily wonder, "Who's he going to encourage to go after *me*?" Ideally, Sarah should tell the two men she was offended by their remarks. But given that one of them is her boss, it would be understandable if she were reluctant to criticize his behavior.

Franklin isn't just romantically interested in Justine; he "has the hots" for her and is willing to "do almost anything" to get a date with her. Justine could well be interested in a "fling" with Franklin. But she's irritated by the sexual remarks and innuendoes in the workplace. It's unlikely that she would be flattered by attention from one of the men responsible for this atmosphere.

Justine can just say no to Franklin. But she may well object to having to say no over and over. And most women are not pleased to be the brunt of jokes and boasts. Some may argue that whether Franklin and Justine get together is a personal matter between the two of them. The moment it becomes the subject of public boasting, however, Franklin's interest in Justine ceases to be just a private interaction.

The law doesn't say Justine should be tough enough to speak up on her own—it says the company is responsible for providing an environment free of offensive or hostile behavior. As the person in charge, the boss ought to know what kind of remarks are being made in the workplace and whether employees are offended by them. Instead of making Franklin think the way to win favor with him is to pressure a coworker into bed, the manager might want to arrange for some training on sexual harassment.

Scenario 2

Freda has been working for Bruce for three years. He believes they have a good working relationship. Freda has never complained to Bruce about anything and appears to be happy in her job. Bruce regularly compliments Freda on her clothing; in his opinion, she has excellent taste and a good figure. Typically, he'll make a remark like "You sure look good today." Last week, Freda was having a bad day and told Bruce that she was "sick and tired of being treated like a sex object." Bruce was stunned. (From the consulting firm of Jane C. Edmonds & Associates, Inc., *Boston Globe*, 10/24/91.)

There's really not enough information to come to any conclusions in this case. The scenario explains how Bruce feels, but not Freda. In the past, when he said, "Hey, you look good today," did Freda usually answer, "So do you"? Or did he murmur, "Mmm, you look go-o-o-o-d," and stare at her chest while she crossed her arms and said, "Thank you, sir"? In addition to complimenting Freda's appearance, did Bruce ever praise her work? Did he compliment other women? men?

It is plausible that Freda might have been upset earlier. She probably wouldn't say she was tired of being treated like a sex object unless she'd felt that way before. Why didn't she speak up sooner? It's not uncommon for someone in Freda's situation to be reluctant to say anything for fear of looking foolish or appearing to be a "bad sport." Remember, Bruce is her boss.

Bruce states that he was stunned when Freda blew up at him. He needs to consider whether Freda might have given him any signals he ignored. He should ask himself how his compliments fit in with the way he treats other employees. Has he really given Freda an opening to object to his remarks?

The most comfortable solution might be for Bruce and Freda to sit down and talk. Perhaps Freda doesn't really mind the compliments themselves but wants more attention paid to her work. If Freda has been upset about the compliments all along, Bruce is probably guilty only of not paying close attention to her feelings. He should let her know that he values her work *and* her feelings, listen carefully to what she has to say, and encourage her to speak up promptly about issues that may arise in the future.

Scenario 3

Barbara is a receptionist for a printing company. Surrounding her desk are five versions of ads printed by the company for a beer distributor. The posters feature women provocatively posed with a can of beer and the slogan, "What'll you have?" On numerous occasions, male customers have walked in, looked at the posters, and commented, "I'll have you, baby." When Barbara tells her boss she wants the posters removed, he responds by saying they represent the company's work and he's proud to display them. He claims no one but Barbara is bothered by the posters.

The legal standard in this case is not how the boss feels, but whether a "reasonable woman" might object to being surrounded by such posters. The company has other products it could display. Barbara has not insisted that the company refuse this account or exclude these posters from the company portfolio. She has merely said she doesn't want the posters displayed around *her* desk. Barbara's view is substantiated by how she's been treated; the posters seem to give customers license to make suggestive remarks to her.

Scenario 4

Therese tells Andrew, her subordinate, that she needs him to escort her to a party. She says she's selecting him because he's the most handsome guy on her staff. Andrew says he's busy. Therese responds that she expects people on her staff to be team players.

Therese may have wanted Andrew merely to accompany her to the party, not to have a sexual relationship with her. And Andrew might have been willing to go along if he hadn't been busy. Nevertheless, a reasonable employee may worry about what the boss means by such a request, particularly when it's coupled with remarks about personal appearance.

Andrew might not mind that Therese finds him handsome. But most people would object to having their job tied to their willingness to make a social appearance with the boss outside of work. The implicit threat also makes Therese's request unacceptable. The company should prohibit managers from requiring subordinates to escort them to social engagements.

Scenario 5

Darlene invites her coworker Dan for a date. They begin a relationship that lasts several months. Then Darlene decides she is no longer interested and breaks up with Dan. He wants the relationship to continue. During the workday, he frequently calls her on the interoffice phone and stops by her desk to talk. Darlene tries to brush him off, but with no success. She asks her manager to intervene. The manager says he doesn't get involved in personal matters.

Most managers are rightly reluctant to involve themselves in employees' personal relationships. Had Darlene asked for help dealing with Dan outside of work, the manager would have been justified in staying out of it. He could have referred her to the employee assistance program, if the company had one.

Once Dan starts interfering with Darlene's work, however, it's a different story. The company has an obligation to make sure the work environment is free from harassment. If Darlene finds herself less able to do her job or uncomfortable at work because of Dan and if her own efforts have failed, the manager has both the right and the responsibility to step in and tell Dan to back off.

Scenario 6

Susan likes to tell bawdy jokes. Bob objects. Although he doesn't mind when men use such language in the office, he doesn't think it's appropriate for women to do so.

An employee who objects to off-color jokes shouldn't have to listen to them at work, and management should back him up. Bob's problem, however, is restricted to jokes told by women. If he doesn't have the same problem when men tell such jokes, it's his problem—not the company's. Management can't enforce Bob's double standard.

Scenario 7

Janet is wearing a low-cut blouse and short shorts. John, her coworker, says, "Now that I can see it, you gotta let me have some." Janet tells him to buzz off. All day, despite Janet's objections, John continues to make similar remarks. When Janet calls her supervisor over to complain, John says, "Hey, can you blame me?"

The company has a right to expect clothing appropriate to the job. If Janet's clothes are inappropriate, management should tell her so. But Janet's outfit doesn't give John license to say or do whatever he likes. Once she tells him she doesn't like his comments, he should stop—or be made to do so.

Scenario 8

Someone posts a Hustler *magazine centerfold in the employee men's room. No women use this room.*

Some would say that if the women aren't aware of the pinups in the men's room, they can't be offensive. But when men walk out of the restroom with such images in their mind's eye, how do they view their female coworkers? And when the women find out about the pinups—as they will—how will they feel? As the judge ruled in a 1991 Florida case involving nude posters at a shipyard, the presence of such pictures, even if they aren't intended to offend women, "sexualizes the work environment to the detriment of all female employees."

A COMMON-SENSE DEFINITION

Sexual harassment is not complicated to define. To harass someone is to bother him or her. Sexual harassment is bothering someone in a sexual way. The harasser offers sexual attention to someone who didn't ask for it and doesn't welcome it. The unwelcome behavior might or might not involve touching. It could just as well be spoken words, graphics, gestures or even looks (not any look—but the kind of leer or stare that says, "I want to undress you").

Who decides what behavior is offensive at the workplace? The recipient does. As long as the recipient is "reasonable" and not unduly sensitive, sexual conduct that offends him or her should be changed.

That doesn't mean there's a blueprint for defining *sexual harassment*. "Reasonable" people don't always agree. Society celebrates pluralism. Not everyone is expected to have the same standards of morality or the same sense of humor. Still, reasonable people will agree *much of the time* about what constitutes offensive behavior or will recognize that certain behavior or language can be expected to offend some others. Most people make distinctions between how they talk to their best friends, to their children, and to their elderly relatives. Out of respect, they avoid certain behavior in the presence of certain people. The same distinctions must be applied at work.

Sexual harassment is different from the innocent mistake—that is, when someone tells an off-color joke, not realizing the listener will be offended, or gives what is meant as a friendly squeeze of the arm to a coworker who doesn't like to be touched. Such behavior may represent insensitivity, and that may be a serious problem, but it's usually not sexual harassment. In many cases, the person who tells the joke that misfires or who pats an unreceptive arm *knows right away* that he or she has made a mistake. Once aware or made aware, this individual will usually apologize and try not to do it again.

DO THEY MEAN IT?

Some offensive behavior stems from what University of Illinois psychologist Louise Fitzgerald calls "cultural lag." "Many men entered the workplace at a time when sexual teasing and innuendo were commonplace," Fitzgerald told the *New York Times*. "They have no idea there's anything wrong with it." Education will help such men change their behavior.

True harassers, on the other hand, *mean* to offend. Even when they know their talk or action is offensive, they continue. Sexual harassment is defined as behavior that is not only unwelcome but *repeated*. (Some kinds of behavior are *always* inappropriate, however, even if they occur only once. Grabbing someone's breast or crotch, for example, or threatening to fire a subordinate who won't engage in sexual activity does not need repetition to be deemed illegal.)

The true harasser acts not out of insensitivity but precisely because of the knowledge that the behavior will make the recipient uncomfortable. The harasser derives pleasure from the momentary or continuing powerlessness of the other individual. In some cases, the harasser presses the victim to have sex, but sexual pleasure itself is not the goal. Instead, the harasser's point is to dominate, to gain power over another. As University of Washington psychologist John Gottman puts it, "Harassment is a way for a man to make a woman vulnerable."

Some harassers target the people they consider the most likely to be embarrassed and least likely to file a charge. Male harassers are sometimes attempting to put "uppity women" in their place. In certain previously all-male workplaces, a woman who's simply attempting to do her job may be considered uppity. In this instance, the harassment is designed to make the woman feel out of place, if not to pressure her out of the job. Such harassment often takes place in front of an audience or is recounted to others afterwards ("pinch and tell").

Dr. Frances Conley, the renowned neurosurgeon who quit her job at Stanford Medical School after nearly 25 years of harassment, told legislators at a sexual harassment hearing in San Diego, California, that the "unsolicited touching, caressing, comments about my physical attributes" she experienced "were always for effect in front of an audience. . . ."

PART OF THE JOB

Some harassers who don't consciously set out to offend are nevertheless unwilling to curb their behavior even after they're told it's offensive. If a woman doesn't like it, they figure that's her problem. And some harassers consider sexual favors from subordinates to be a "perk," as much a part of the job as a big mahogany desk and a private executive bathroom. A young woman on President Lyndon Johnson's staff, according to *A Sexual Profile of Men in Power* (Prentice-Hall, 1977), by Sam Janus and others, "was awakened in her bedroom on his Texas ranch in the middle of the night by a searching flashlight. Before she could scream, she heard a familiar voice: 'Move over. This is your president.'"

Men can be harassed by women, or both harasser and victim can be of the same sex. Overwhelmingly, however, sexual harassment is an injury inflicted on women by men. While the number of hardcore harassers is small, their presence is widely felt. Sexual harassment is ugly. And it's damaging—to the victims, to business, and to society as a whole.

DEFINING SEXUAL HARASSMENT

Sexual harassment means bothering someone in a sexual way.

Sexual harassment is behavior that is not only unwelcome but in most cases *repeated*.

The goal of sexual harassment is not sexual pleasure but gaining power over another.

Some male harassers want to put "uppity women" in their place.

The essence of combating sexual harassment is fostering mutual respect in the workplace.

2

Countering the Myths about Sexual Harassment

From the Senate chambers to the company mailroom, from the executive suite to the employee lounge, from the locker room to the bedroom, a debate is raging over sexual harassment. No matter what the forum, the same arguments arise. Here are some of the most common myths about harassment rebutted by the facts.

Myth: Sexual harassment doesn't deserve all the attention it's getting. It's a rare disorder unique to a few sick people.

Fact: No exact figures exist, but a large body of research conducted at workplaces and universities suggests that at least 50 percent of women—as well as a smaller percentage of men—have been sexually harassed, either on the job or on campus. Very few people are considered to be "chronic harassers," but most of these are not psychopaths. Many men in the workplace, whether intentionally or not, end up encouraging or condoning harassment.

Myth: Sexual harassment is a fact of life that people might as well get used to. It's so widespread that it's pointless to try to stamp it out.

Fact: To expect men to engage in abusive behavior is insulting. The notion that women should take responsibility for preventing harassers from behaving offensively at the workplace is also a myth. Like other forms of sexual abuse, harassment is usually a means of exerting power, not of expressing a biological urge. Yes, sexual harassment is widespread, but the answer is to stop it, not to accept it.

Myth: Most men accused of harassment don't really intend to offend women.

Fact: A small percentage of men are dead serious about engaging in abusive behavior on the job. They know their behavior makes women uncomfortable; that's why they do it.

Other men are surprised to find that what they intend as innocent teasing isn't received that way. They need to make some simple changes in behavior. After all, beginning in early childhood, most people are taught that different settings require different codes of behavior. Children learn not to use swear words at Grandma's dinner table and not to insult the teacher. At the workplace, it's safest to assume that a coworker *won't* like sexual comments or gestures. If you find out you've offended someone, simply apologize.

Myth: If women want to be treated equally on the job, they can't expect special treatment—whether at the construction site or in the executive boardroom.

Fact: Women don't want special treatment. They want *decent* treatment—the same decent treatment most men want for themselves.

As for the use of profane language on the job, an Illinois judge developed a rule known as the "stub-your-toe test" designed to distinguish simple expletives from words that demean women. If you stubbed your toe, the judge asks, would you yell, "Oh, cunt!"?

Myth: Many charges of sexual harassment are false—the women are either fantasizing or lying in order to get men in trouble.

Fact: According to a survey of Fortune 500 managers conducted by *Working Woman* magazine (December 1988), false reports are rare. "Every story I hear is very specific and very detailed," said one survey respondent, "too much so to be made up." Said another respondent, "More than 95 percent of our complaints have merit."

There's little incentive for women to come forward with false harassment charges. The real problem is not that reports are fraudulent but that women who *are* suffering severe harassment remain silent for fear of being humiliated and derailing their careers.

Myth: A man's career can be destroyed by an accusation of sexual harassment, while the woman who accuses him suffers no consequences.

Fact: A woman's *life* can be destroyed by sexual harassment, at least for a time. Offensive behavior *should* bring consequences for the perpetrator. But most cases don't result in heavy penalties.

A good corporate policy, however, protects both the accuser and the accused by ensuring confidentiality and a fair hearing. A range of disciplinary action is needed—from warnings and reprimands to suspensions and terminations—depending on the severity of the offense.

As things stand now, it's usually the victim who suffers a career setback. Many harassers receive only a slap on the wrist or no reprisals at all, even for serious offenses.

Myth: You can't blame a guy for looking. Women bring harassment on themselves by the way they dress.

Fact: Truly provocative clothing doesn't belong at the workplace, and management shouldn't allow it. Yet under no circumstances does a woman's appearance give men license to break the law.

Many employers require women to dress in a way that calls attention to their physical appearance. Waitresses, for example, may be required to wear uniforms with short skirts or low necklines. In 1991, Continental Airlines reservation clerk Teresa Fischette was summarily fired when she refused to wear makeup on the job. Only after the *New York Times* publicized her case and she appeared on a television talk show did she win back her position.

Without questioning the importance of being well groomed, many women resent having to conform to a highly specific "look" for the benefit of clients or coworkers. Not only is it expensive and time-consuming, it can lead others to treat them like sex objects at the workplace.

Myth: Women send mixed signals. Half the time when they say no, they really mean yes.

Fact: Men can't assume they're the ones who know best what women "really want." Especially at the workplace, some women can't put up strong resistance to sexual pressure without fear of endangering their jobs. Dr. Michelle Paludi, a psychologist at Hunter College in New York City, finds that "90 percent of women who have been sexually harassed want to leave, but can't because they need their job." Take a no as a no.

Myth: Women who make clear that they don't welcome sexual attention don't get harassed. If a woman doesn't like what's happening, she can say so.

Fact: Most hard-core harassers know their conduct is unwelcome; that's why they continue. Some women do say no again and again and find that their resistance is simply ignored. Others hesitate to speak up because they fear being ridiculed or ostracized.

While women do have a responsibility to communicate when sexual attention is unwelcome, the employer has a prior legal responsibility: to create an environment where no woman is punished for refusing to accept offensive behavior.

Myth: All this attention to harassment will give women ideas, causing them to imagine problems where there are none.

Fact: In the short run, defining *sexual harassment* and providing women with ways to speak up probably *will* lead to an increase in the number of reports filed, most of them concerning legitimate, not imagined, offenses. In the long run, however, public discussion of the issue will cut down on unwelcome sexual attention on the job. The result will be fewer harassment complaints and a more harmonious and productive work world for all.

Myth: Cracking down on sexual harassment will lead to a boring and humorless workplace.

Fact: Antiharassment policies are aimed at repeated, unwelcome sexual attention, not at friendly relations among coworkers. Social interaction that's mutually enjoyable is fine, so long as it doesn't interfere with work or offend others.

The aim of a sexual-harassment policy is to eliminate *offensive* interactions, not *all* interactions. Most encounters defined as sexual harassment have nothing to do with a romantic agenda. They involve an assertion of power, not of affection.

But sex between managers and their subordinates—or between faculty and students—is a different story. Many employers and college administrators recognize that romantic relationships are fraught with danger when one party to the affair has economic or academic power over the other. Even when it seems that both parties have entered freely into the relationship, management is right to worry about the potential for exploitation and adverse effects on the workplace or academic setting.

The University of Iowa forbids faculty-student relationships with these words:

> Voluntary consent by the student in such a relationship is suspect, given the fundamentally asymmetric nature of the relationship. Moreover, other students and faculty may be affected by such unprofessional behavior because it places the faculty member in a position to favor or advance one student's interest at the expense of others and implicitly makes obtaining benefits contingent on amorous or sexual favors. Therefore, the University will view it as unethical if faculty members engage in amorous relations with students enrolled in their classes or subject to their supervision, even when both parties appear to have consented to the relationship. (University of Iowa Office of Affirmative Action, Iowa City, Iowa)

FACTS ABOUT SEXUAL HARASSMENT

At least 50 percent of women, and a smaller percentage of men, have been harassed on the job or on campus.

It's safest to assume that a coworker *won't* enjoy sexual comments or gestures.

Management should provide a work environment that is free of harassment for all employees.

False accusations of sexual harassment are rare. A good policy protects both the accuser and the accused by ensuring confidentiality and a fair hearing.

Women have a responsibility to communicate when sexual attention is unwelcome. But employers have a prior responsibility to ensure that no woman is punished for refusing to accept offensive behavior.

3

What the Law Says

What words would you use to describe sexual harassment? Participants in workplace training sessions are always full of answers. "Humiliating," they call out. "Unwelcome." "Repeated." "Power abuse." The list goes on. Yet in session after session, at one workplace after another, no one but the instructor states a word that's just as important as all the rest: *illegal*. Sexual harassment is against the law.

It's not surprising that most people are uninformed about the law on sexual harassment. Not until 1977 did a federal court uphold a harassment charge. The Supreme Court did not do so until 1986. Until a short time ago, sexual harassment was a problem without a name or a remedy.

Employees and employers alike can be thankful that sexual harassment is unlawful. Those who use the laws to file charges aren't the only ones who benefit. For *all* employees, simply knowing they have a right to a harassment-free workplace makes it easier to insist on fair treatment. For many potential harassers, the laws are an effective deterrent. And for employers seeking to enforce appropriate workplace behavior, the laws are invaluable.

In recent years, state and federal rulemakers and a series of court cases have steadily clarified and strengthened the law. In the future, a better legal process may do even more to prevent harassment, protect the victim, and punish the harasser.

FEDERAL LAW DEFINES HARASSMENT

Title VII of the Civil Rights Act of 1964 makes it illegal to discriminate against employees on the basis of race, color, religion, sex, or national origin. As enforced by the Equal Employment Opportunity Commission (EEOC), the law gives every employee the right to work in an environment free of intimidation, insult, or ridicule based on race, religion, or sex.

Here's how the EEOC, a Washington-based agency with regional offices, defines *sexual harassment*:

> Unwelcome sexual advances, requests for sexual favors, and other verbal or physical conduct of a sexual nature constitute sexual harassment when
>
> 1. submission to such conduct is made either explicitly or implicitly a *term or condition of an individual's employment* or academic advancement,
> 2. submission to or rejection of such conduct by an individual is used as the *basis for employment decisions* or academic decisions affecting such individual, or
> 3. such conduct has the purpose or effect of unreasonably *interfering with an individual's work* or academic performance or creating an intimidating, *hostile*, or offensive working or academic *environment*.

Illegal sexual harassment falls into four categories: *quid pro quo*, hostile environment, sexual favoritism, and harassment by nonemployees.

Quid Pro Quo

Quid pro quo means something given in return for something else. In this type of sexual harassment, a supervisor makes unwelcome sexual advances and either states or implies that the victim *must* submit if she wants to keep her job or receive a raise, promotion, or job assignment.

These cases are the most clear-cut. The courts generally hold the employer liable for any such harassment, whether he knew about it or not. That's because anyone who holds a supervisory position, with power over terms of employment, is considered to be an "agent" of the employer, that is, "acting for" the employer.

Deborah, an office manager at a small firm, couldn't stop Bill, the sales and marketing manager, from coming by her desk to complain about his unsatisfying sex life with his wife. She insisted again and again that she wasn't interested in hearing about his personal affairs, but nothing she said would deter him. Finally, Deborah went to their boss for help. "Put your faith in God," was all he had to say. Deborah did her best to avoid Bill, but then a corporate restructuring took place and he became president of the firm. "I'm on the other side of the desk now," he told Deborah in their first meeting. "Either we engage in a sexual relationship, or I no longer need an office manager." Deborah filed a charge and won.

Hostile Environment

An employee doesn't have to be fired, demoted, or denied a raise or promotion to be "harmed"—and to file a charge. Even if no threat is involved, unwelcome sexual conduct can have the effect of "poisoning" the victim's work environment. Sexually explicit jokes, pinups, graffiti, vulgar statements, abusive language, innuendoes, and overt sexual conduct can create a hostile environment.

In these cases, the employer is considered liable if he knew or should have known of the harassment and did nothing to stop it. If the harassment is out in the open, if everyone except the employer knows all about it, then he *ought* to have known—whether or not anyone brings the matter to his attention.

Where no *quid pro quo* is involved, the courts generally don't rule in favor of the victim unless the incidents of harassment are repeated, pervasive, and harmful to the victim's emotional well-being. A single incident isn't enough to prove the existence of a hostile environment, unless the incident is extreme. An employer can let a vulgar remark or two go by without being found in violation of the law. But if someone intentionally *touches* an employee in a sexual way on the job even once and the employer ignores the behavior, then the EEOC will generally find that harassment has occurred.

Hostile environment cases may leave more room for argument than *quid pro quo* cases.

The victim will strengthen his or her case by complaining or protesting at the time of the harassment, preferably in writing. This kind of documentation will prove that the victim finds the sexual attention unwelcome—and will also help prove that the offensive behavior occurred in the first place, if the employer is inclined to deny it.

But a verbal or written protest is not absolutely necessary to winning a case—the EEOC recognizes that it's not always possible to speak up. Even if the employer claims, as a defense, that there was a grievance procedure and the victim never used it, the EEOC will examine what may have deterred the victim from doing so. How often has the grievance procedure been used? Do all employees know it exists? Have other harassment victims felt comfortable using it?

Carol Zabkowicz, a warehouse worker, was tormented by a group of male coworkers who enjoyed upsetting her by calling out her name and then exposing their genitals or buttocks when she looked up. Carol complained to management, to no avail. "If we didn't see it, it didn't happen" was the company's position. Even when she brought witnesses with her and submitted evidence in the form of obscene cartoons that had been left at her workstation, management did nothing. When the case went to court, the company was found guilty of "malicious, blatant discrimination."

The employer's best defense will be to take the strong preventive and remedial action recommended in the EEOC's guidelines:

The employer should affirmatively raise the subject with all supervisory and nonsupervisory employees, express strong disapproval, and explain the sanctions for harassment. The employer should also have a procedure for resolving sexual harassment complaints. The procedure should be designed to encourage victims of harassment to come forward and should not require a victim to complain first to the offending supervisor. It should ensure confidentiality as much as possible and provide effective remedies and protection of victims and witnesses against retaliation.

If the employer takes strong action immediately upon finding out about a "hostile environment" problem, the EEOC may find that the situation has been resolved satisfactorily and close the case, even if the harassment is as severe as in this example:

A foreman at a factory grabbed a woman employee and forced her face against his crotch. She left the scene crying while he and other male workers laughed. After the woman complained, management reprimanded the foreman and denied him a promotion and a merit increase. The woman filed a charge at the EEOC. But because the employer had quickly disciplined the offender, the agency denied the woman's claim.

If, on the other hand, the employer had done nothing but tell the woman to forget about the foreman's offensive behavior, the EEOC would almost certainly have found him to be discriminating against the victim by giving tacit support to the harasser.

Sexual Favoritism

In this type of harassment, a supervisor rewards only those employees who submit to sexual demands. The *other* employees, those who are *denied* raises or promotions, can claim that they're penalized by the sexual attention directed at the favored coworkers.

Catherine A. Broderick, an attorney with the federal Securities and Exchange Commission, filed a suit charging that the agency was run "like a brothel." Senior attorneys were having affairs with secretaries and junior attorneys and rewarding them with cash bonuses and promotions. When Broderick complained, she received poor reviews and was threatened with firing. She won her case, receiving $128,000 in back pay and a promotion.

Harassment by Nonemployees

An employer can be held responsible for harassment by people outside the company—such as customers, vendors, or contractors—if the employer has control or could have control over their actions.

The owner of an office building required a female elevator operator to wear a sexy uniform. People riding the elevator made lewd remarks and propositioned her. The operator complained to the owner and said she refused to wear the uniform. For this she was fired. She brought suit against the employer and won.

HARASSMENT OF MEN; SAME-SEX HARASSMENT

Sexual harassment of men by women is also illegal, though considerably less common than harassment of women by men. The female supervisor who repeatedly pressures her male employee for dates is engaging in illegal harassment. In 1989, a Michigan man won a jury award after a group of female coworkers wrote him sexually provocative notes and fondled his buttocks.

The law also covers situations where employees are subjected to unwelcome sexual attention from someone of the same sex. A male supervisor, for example, may not legally pressure a male employee for sexual favors.

At this time, however, homosexuals who are intimidated or

insulted because of their sexual orientation aren't protected by federal law. If a group of workers tormented a gay employee by making effeminate gestures in his presence or calling him a "fairy" or if a supervisor made a point of telling demeaning jokes about homosexuals in order to "tease" a lesbian employee, the EEOC would not consider such actions to be sex discrimination.

Unlike federal law, a small number of state and local statutes do protect homosexuals from discrimination. Call your state or local fair-employment agency for more information.

THE LEGAL HISTORY OF SEXUAL HARASSMENT

The legal history of sexual harassment is surprisingly short. Not until 1964 was sex discrimination itself declared illegal—and only by a fluke. During the debate over the proposed Civil Rights Act at that time, a Southern member of Congress proposed what he considered an absurd amendment, making sex discrimination illegal along with race discrimination. His intent was only to make sure the bill wouldn't pass; to his chagrin, however, the plan backfired. The bill became law with his amendment intact, and discrimination on the basis of sex as well as race was outlawed.

Eight years later, in 1972, Congress passed the Equal Employment Opportunity Act giving enforcement powers to the EEOC. That same year, President Nixon signed the Education Amendments, forbidding discrimination by any education program receiving federal funds.

The First Cases of Sexual Harassment

In the mid-1970s, the first sexual harassment cases began to make their way through the courts. The victims lost.

- In *Corne v. Bausch & Lomb,* two Arizona women who worked for a manufacturer of eye-care products resigned because of harassment by a supervisor. According to the court, the harassment was a "personal peculiarity" of the supervisor for which the employer couldn't be held responsible.

- Diane Williams, an information officer for the Justice Department, was fired nine days after refusing her supervisor's sexual advances. In an important victory, a lower court awarded her $16,000—but the Justice Department appealed and won.

- In *Miller v. Bank of America*, the court found the harassment was "isolated misconduct," not the employer's responsibility. (In 1979, the Ninth Circuit reversed this ruling.)

First Academic Case Filed

In 1977, students brought charges of sexual harassment for the first time under Title IX of the 1972 Education Amendments. An undergraduate student at Yale University charged that her professor propositioned her, promising her an *A* in his course in she would accept his advances. She refused and received a *C*. The woman filed charges along with four other students and a faculty member. (Three years later, *Alexander v. Yale* was dismissed. By then the student had graduated and Yale had established a grievance procedure for harassment victims.)

Harassment Ruled Illegal Sex Discrimination

Finally, in the precedent-setting *Barnes v. Costle* case, sexual harassment victims gained a foothold in the courts. The U.S. Court of Appeals for the District of Columbia ruled in 1977 in favor of a woman whose government job was abolished because she wouldn't submit to her boss's demand for sexual favors. "But for her womanhood," the court said, "the woman wouldn't have lost her job." If she'd been a man, in other words, she wouldn't have been treated this way. Therefore, the harassment was not just an isolated instance of supervisory misbehavior; it was illegal sex discrimination.

EEOC Guidelines Established

More progress was seen in 1980. More than 15 years after the passage of Title VII, under the leadership of Chairwoman Eleanor Holmes Norton, the EEOC finally published guidelines stating specifically that sexual harassment was a form of sex discrimination and encouraging employers to take positive steps to prevent it. Later that year, a transition committee for the newly elected Reagan Administration recommended that these guidelines be rescinded. (Future Supreme Court Justice Clarence Thomas, by the way, was a member of the committee.) In 1981, the U.S. Senate held hearings chaired by Sen. Orrin G. Hatch (R-Utah) to consider whether the guidelines were antibusiness. Despite these challenges, the guidelines survived.

In 1982, the EEOC ruled that one woman's word was inadequate to prove sexual harassment—in the absence of a corroborating witness, the alleged harasser would prevail. (The agency ruled differently the following year.)

Hostile Environment: An Uphill Battle

While the concept of *quid pro quo* harassment was accepted by courts in the 1970s, victims of hostile environment harassment fought an uphill battle in the 1980s.

Deep Throat Allowed at Hospital Meeting

In 1986, a jury in a Missouri court rejected a $4-million suit brought by Olivia Young, a medical-services saleswoman who was shown the pornographic movie *Deep Throat* at a meeting at a St. Louis hospital.

Explicit Posters Allowed

In *Rabidue v. Osceola Refining Co.*, an administrative assistant sued over the presence of posters of naked women at her workplace. One poster depicted a woman lying down with a golf ball on her breasts, straddled by a man holding a golf club. A supervisor frequently called women employees "whores," "cunt," "pussy," and "tits." He once said of the victim, "All that bitch needs is a good lay." The federal appeals court in Cincinnati ruled in 1986 against the victim, deciding that she wasn't the kind of person who would find such conduct unwelcome. Further, said the court, since erotica is displayed at newsstands and in other public places, there's no way to restrict it at the workplace.

1986: The Supreme Court Recognizes Hostile Environment Harassment

At last, in June 1986, the Supreme Court upheld the concept of *hostile environment harassment*. In *Meritor Savings Bank v. Vinson*, the court affirmed that harassment is illegal even if the victim hasn't lost any job benefits—even if it's not a *quid pro quo* situation. Employees have "the right to work in an environment free from discriminatory intimidation, ridicule, and insult," the Court said.

Mechelle Vinson, a bank teller who worked her way up to a position as an assistant branch manager, claimed that her supervisor repeatedly pressured her to have sex with him. At first she resisted; finally, afraid of losing her job, she gave in to his advances. Over the next several years, he fondled her in front of other employees, followed her into the restroom, and exposed himself at work. He had sex with her 40 or 50 times and raped her on more than one occasion. Finally, she went on leave and was fired. Her employer's defense was that she'd made up the whole story, dressed provocatively, and never used the grievance procedure.

Voluntary?

The lower court found that if there was a sexual relationship between Vinson and her supervisor, it was a voluntary one, and that the employer wasn't liable because Vinson hadn't complained. But the court of appeals disagreed. Even though Vinson had indeed agreed to have sex with the supervisor, said the court, her participation couldn't fairly be called "voluntary" because she was afraid she'd lose her job if she refused. Further, regardless of whether she had lodged a complaint, the bank was liable because a supervisor is an agent of the employer.

The bank appealed to the Supreme Court, which affirmed the court of appeals. The Court said that the question was not whether Vinson had made a voluntary decision to have sex with her supervisor, but whether the sexual relationship was welcome or unwelcome to her.

The Court also asserted that merely having a sexual harassment policy and a grievance procedure didn't automatically excuse the employer from liability. But the Court didn't go so far as to say that employers were always liable for the actions of supervisors. Where no *quid pro quo* threats are made, the Court said, the employer's liability must be determined on a case-by-case basis.

The Case of the Reasonable Woman

It's common practice in the courtroom to examine behavior through the eyes of the hypothetical "reasonable person," the so-called "man in the street." But in 1991, in *Ellison v. Brady*, the U.S. Court of Appeals for the Ninth Circuit created a new standard: the "reasonable woman."

Kerry Ellison, an agent for the Internal Revenue Service in San Mateo, California, charged that a coworker persisted in pressuring her for dates even though she kept refusing him. He sent her bizarre "love letters" that she found frightening. "I know that you are worth knowing with or without sex," said one letter. "I have enjoyed you so much over the past few months. Watching you. Experiencing you from so far away." When Ellison complained to a supervisor, the coworker was transferred. He filed a grievance, however, and won a return to Ellison's office. At this point, Ellison filed a harassment charge.

A district court dismissed the case, calling the coworker's conduct "isolated and genuinely trivial." But the Ninth Circuit of the U.S. Court of Appeals disagreed. The "severe and pervasive" harassment directed at Ellison, the court wrote, had created "an abusive working environment." And while IRS managers told the coworker to stop his illegal harassment, they didn't subject him to any disciplinary action—no reprimand, no probation, no threat of termination. They even decided to transfer him back to Ellison's office without consulting her.

In the court's view, the reasonable-person standard could end up simply reinforcing discrimination. After all, if harassment is common and widespread, doesn't it follow that an average, "reasonable" person can engage in harassment? Fairness demands that the law take note of women's unique perspective. The court wrote:

> Conduct that many men consider unobjectionable may offend many women. Because women are disproportionately victims of rape and sexual assault, women have a stronger incentive to be concerned with sexual behavior. Women who are victims of mild forms of sexual harassment may understandably worry whether a harasser's conduct is merely a prelude to a violent sexual assault. Men, who are rarely victims of sexual assault, may view sexual conduct in a vacuum without a full appreciation of the social setting or the underlying threat of violence that a woman may perceive.

Robinson v. Jacksonville Shipyards: Workplace Pornography Banned

Another breakthrough came in 1991. For the first time, a court ruled that pornography at the workplace constituted sex discrimination.

Lois Robinson, a welder, was one of only six women among over 800 skilled craftworkers at a Florida shipyard. When female employees reported demeaning jokes and comments to managers, their complaints were not taken seriously. In addition, pictures of nude women were displayed—sometimes by managers— throughout the workplace. One pinup showed a meat spatula pressed against a woman's pubic area. Another picture featured a nude woman holding a whip. A drawing on the wall featured a nude woman's body with "USDA Choice" stamped across it as if it were a piece of meat. Graffiti—"eat me," "pussy"—were scrawled on the walls. And a dartboard was decorated with a drawing of a woman's breast, with the nipple as the bull's-eye.

The district court upheld Robinson's harassment charge, finding that pornography may be far more threatening to women in the workplace than it is outside. "Pornography on an employer's wall or desk communicates a message about the way he views women, a view strikingly at odds with the way women wish to be viewed in the workplace," the court decision declared. Further, "a preexisting atmosphere that deters women from entering or continuing in a profession or job" is as bad as "a sign declaring 'Men Only.'"

The shipyard was ordered to remove the offensive pictures and to implement an antiharassment policy drafted by the National Organization for Women Legal Defense and Education Fund. Two employees were held personally liable for harassment, and the company was ordered to pay Robinson's legal fees, as well as $1 in damages.

An Abridgment of Free Speech?

The employer, with the approval of the American Civil Liberties Union, protested that being forced to remove the posters and graffiti would mean abridging employees' freedom of speech. But many women's groups strongly backed the court's ruling. The messages contained in the pornographic posters would be called sexual harassment—and declared illegal—if they were stated out loud at the workplace. Why should pictures be allowed to convey what workers aren't allowed to say on the job? The "right" of supervisors and male workers to express themselves offensively before a captive audience of female workers must be balanced against other goals, like avoiding discrimination and getting the work done.

Employees Protest Sexually Oriented Ads

Later in 1991, five women employees at Stroh Brewery in St. Paul, Minnesota, raised an issue related to the Jacksonville Shipyards case. They filed a suit charging that the beer company's sex-oriented advertisements—which showed bikini-clad women parachuting into an all-male campsite—contributed to an atmosphere of severe harassment at the plant, where walls were covered with posters of spread-eagled women and a supervisor had once ripped the blouse off an employee. In March 1992, the company withdrew the ads.

Victims Win Right to Collect Damages Under Federal Law

Until the end of 1991, federal law didn't allow harassment victims—or victims of any other form of sex discrimination—to collect much money. All they could win under Title VII were remedies that would make them "whole"—reinstatement if they'd been fired, a promotion if they'd been denied one, back pay, and attorney's fees. There were no remedies for out-of-pocket expenses like medical bills or for emotional pain and suffering. Nor was there any way to assess punitive damages against the employer.

Under the circumstances, many harassment victims saw little reason to sue under Title VII, especially if they didn't want their job back or hadn't been fired in the first place. They couldn't collect a penny, nor would their employer suffer any significant consequences. Victims also found it difficult to interest attorneys in their cases, since there was no chance of collecting damages, even if they won.

In 1991, however, in the wake of Anita Hill's testimony on sexual harassment before the Senate Judiciary Committee, Congress passed legislation strengthening several aspects of civil rights law. The Civil Rights Act of 1991 gives victims of sex, race, and religious discrimination the right to sue for both *compensatory* and *punitive* damages. Victims can sue to collect compensation for the abuse they've suffered, as well as to collect penalties designed to punish the employer. This makes it easier for victims to interest attorneys in taking their cases on a contingent-fee basis. (The lawyer receives little or no payment up front but takes a percentage of the total award, if any, once the case is resolved.) Out-of-pocket medical expenses can now be recovered as well. Further, the law gives the right to trial by jury, and juries are generally acknowledged to be more sympathetic to the victim than judges.

In February 1992, the Supreme Court affirmed that Title IX of the Education Amendments of 1972 gives students the right to recover damages from schools and school officials for sexual harassment and other forms of sex discrimination.

A Step Forward, But . . .

The Civil Rights Act of 1991 is a significant step forward for victims. In some ways, however, it falls short. For sex discrimination, allowable damages are capped at $50,000 for companies with fewer than 101 workers, $100,000 for companies with 101 to 200 workers, $200,000 for companies with 201 to 500 workers, and $300,000 for larger companies. Critics argue that these caps on damages unfairly penalize women. Furthermore, the law still doesn't require employers to take steps to prevent sexual harassment unless specific incidents have already occurred.

It's still unknown how judges and juries will decide what level of damages to award. Presumably, they'll consider the length of time during which the harassment took place, the efforts the victim made to stop it, and the form the harassment took. Physical contact will probably be considered more serious than offensive language.

Class Action

In December 1991, a federal judge in Minneapolis for the first time ever agreed to approve a class-action sexual harassment case. Previously, claims had been pursued only on behalf of individuals. This ruling, involving women mine workers in Duluth, Minnesota, recognized that in certain cases harassment may be so pervasive that it affects a whole group of women.

STATE FAIR-EMPLOYMENT AGENCIES

The EEOC covers only workplaces with 15 or more employees. Harassment victims who work in places with fewer than 15 employees can file charges with fair-employment agencies on the state or local level, as can the employees of larger companies. (For more information, consult your telephone book listings for state or local government.) Some state statutes against sexual harassment are stronger than the federal law. The State of Maine, for example, requires employers to post a sexual harassment policy and provide antiharassment training to new employees. Some state laws allow unlimited damage awards. As with the EEOC, victims don't need a lawyer to file a charge with a state agency.

STATE TORT LAWS

Harassment victims can also file suit under state tort laws—if they can afford to hire a lawyer. A victim who was pressured for dates and tormented by offensive conduct could claim *intentional infliction of emotional distress* (the most common of these claims, but difficult to prove). A victim who was touched without permission could sue on the basis of *assault and battery*. If the harassment made her unable to have sex with her husband, she could claim *loss of consortium*. An employee subjected to offensive behavior in her supervisor's office could claim *false imprisonment*. One whose boss asked her questions about her sex life could claim *invasion of privacy*.

Tort laws have longer statutes of limitations than do the EEOC and local agencies—one to three years instead of a year or less. And tort laws can allow for bigger damage awards (although they also require a greater burden of proof). Some victims have collected substantial amounts. Among recent high awards, according to Jury Verdict Research, Inc., of Ohio, are these:

- *Moore v. Cardinal Services, Inc.:* A woman claimed that a supervisor forced her to perform oral sex by threatening her with the loss of her job. Award: $3.1 million.

- *Bihun v. AT&T Information Systems:* A personnel manager went on leave for emotional distress that she said was caused by the unwelcome advances of her supervisor. While she was out, her job was eliminated and she was transferred to another position with the same pay. Award: $2 million.

- *Preston v. Douglas:* A police officer claimed that coworkers turned on her after she rejected her commander's advances. She was hospitalized for emotional distress. Award: $900,000.

Such large awards are very unusual, however. Most harassment victims receive little in damages from tort actions. In fact, *most* sexual harassment cases, whether filed at the EEOC, at state agencies, or in court, never make it to trial. Those that do tend to involve outrageous conduct, substantial damage to the victim, and very strong evidence.

OTHER LEGAL AVENUES

Harassment victims also have these protections:

- *U.S. Constitution.* The equal protection clause of the Fourteenth Amendment of the United States Constitution can be used by public employees as the basis of a sexual harassment suit.

- *Unemployment Compensation.* In some states, employees who quit or are fired because of sexual harassment can collect unemployment compensation benefits. In other states, no employee who leaves a job "voluntarily" can collect.

- *National Labor Relations Act.* Employees who organize meetings, petitions, letter-writing drives, or other activities to try to improve sexual harassment policies at the workplace are protected by the National Labor Relations Act.

BIAS IN THE COURTROOM

Victims who go to court seeking enforcement of the law sometimes encounter the same bias they experienced on the job, but this time from judges.

Appearance Counts Against Victim

Katherine Young, who worked for a hotel chain, claimed her boss had fired her for refusing his advances. Alabama Judge E.B. Haltom ruled against her. The boss couldn't possibly have been interested in harassing Young, the judge noted, because unlike the boss's wife, Young "wore little or no makeup, and her hair was not colored in any way."

Harasser as Affectionate Protector

Karen Kouri, a personnel assistant at an insurance firm, claimed that her recently divorced boss massaged her, sent her 37 affectionate notes in one three-week period, and followed her to the bathroom. Federal District Judge James C. Cacheris ruled in 1991 that the boss's actions did *not* constitute harassment or threatening behavior. Rather, the boss was merely like a "faithful dog, . . . protective . . ., constantly expressing his affection."

If It's Not Rape, Is It Sexual Harassment?

A woman went to court claiming that a pervasive atmosphere of harassment existed at the paper company where she worked. A coworker had broadcast obscene remarks about her over the public address system. A supervisor had pinched her buttocks with pliers. She'd received dozens of pornographic messages in her locker. Sexually explicit pictures and graffiti, some of it directed at her, adorned the walls and the elevator. After three years of complaining to management with no results, the woman finally resigned. Judge Edith H. Jones listened as the woman's attorney described one offensive incident after another. "Well," the judge finally interrupted to say, "your client wasn't raped."

THE LAW EVOLVES

Despite the few big-money settlements that have grabbed headlines and the steady progress in court decisions, both the law and the enforcement system still pose formidable obstacles for the victim of harassment. The burden is on the victim to prove both that harassment took place and that the offender's conduct was unwelcome. Too often, the courtroom inquiry tends to focus not on what the offender did but on how the victim responded—how strongly she resisted, how quickly she protested, how sincere her objections were. Frequently, judges and juries fail to recognize how hard it is to speak up against harassment if the offender is your boss.

As new statutes are passed and new cases decided, sexual harassment law continues to evolve. In coming years, strides may be made toward more effectively preventing harassment, protecting the victim, and imposing appropriate penalties on harasser and employer.

SEXUAL HARASSMENT IS ILLEGAL

Title VII of the Civil Rights Act of 1964 prohibits discrimination against employees on the basis of race, color, religion, sex, or national origin. As enforced by the Equal Employment Opportunity Commission (EEOC), the law gives every employee the right to work in an environment free of intimidation, insult, or ridicule based on race, religion, or sex.

A sexual harassment charge was first upheld by a federal court in 1977 and by the Supreme Court in 1986.

If a supervisor demands sexual favors and threatens the victim's job, the employer is held responsible.

The victim will strengthen his or her case by complaining or protesting at the time of harassment, if possible—preferably in writing.

A 1991 court recognized that women may be threatened or offended by conduct men don't mind and said workplace behavior should meet the "reasonable woman" standard.

Harassment victims have the right to collect compensatory and punitive damages under the Civil Rights Act of 1991.

4

Effects of Sexual Harassment

Victims of sexual harassment are like victims of a crime. Except that crime victims get empathy—and sexual harassment victims get accusations and scrutiny. Crime victims may have broken locks or a broken arm—but sexual harassment victims have a broken spirit for many years.

Diane Donelson, City of Omaha, Nebraska, Employee Assistance Program

Women who are defending themselves physically and emotionally will find it hard to build the trust on which effective teamwork depends. That's why the barriers erected by sexual harassment drain valuable energy from the workplace—just when we need the very most every team member can contribute.

Faith Wohl, Director, Work Force Partnering, Du Pont Company

Think of sexual harassment as a house on fire in a crowded neighborhood. Left to burn out of control, the fire can spread and destroy other houses as well. And even houses that escape the flames may be damaged by smoke and water. It will take a long time for the block to return to normal.

For the victim, sexual harassment can have serious psychological, physical, and economic effects—effects that easily compound each other. But seldom does harassment affect the victim alone. In severe cases, it can devastate that person's family. And even minor instances of harassment can harm a company in many ways, both immediate and long-term.

PSYCHOLOGICAL EFFECTS

Victims of sexual harassment can experience a wide range of emotional reactions, from self-doubt and self-blame to severe depression. Suffering the harassment is bad enough. But victims also have to deal with society's ignorance. Employers, friends, and family members all tend to minimize the damage. And psychological distress itself can lead to physical illness, deteriorated performance, lost work time, and unexpected expenses.

Self-Doubt

Many people who experience sexual harassment are bewildered and confused at first. It's hard for them to believe that someone in a position of authority or trust would treat them so badly. Even when they recognize what's happening, women often think they should be strong enough to handle it on their own.

"Is It Me?" Lois worked as a claims adjuster at an insurance company. Harley, her boss, made unwelcome sexual comments and showed pornographic pictures to her and other employees. No one ever said anything about Harley's behavior, and for a long time Lois remained silent herself.

Lois described her reactions in an interview with 9to5: "You think, is there something wrong with me? Am I different because I perceive this differently? Is there something wrong with my sense of humor? Why aren't other people incensed?"

"Hang In There" Anna, an engineer, experienced harassment at the hands of her boss for several months. "My common sense told me that I could not continue like this," she said, "but my pride told me to keep working at it. You're tough, kid, keep fighting."

Later, Anna decided to confront her boss. She secretly taped the conversation with a recorder stashed in her boot. "When I transcribed the tape," she said, "I heard myself trying to console this man. I was feeling sorry for the man who was trying to force me out of my job."

Denial and Self-Blame

Few sexual harassment victims know their legal rights or seek help right away. At least at first, most tend to deny what is happening ("I must be imagining it") or blame themselves ("I must have done something to cause it").

"If I Just Work Hard Enough" Patricia Kidd, an organizer of office space for District of Columbia employees, endured constant pressure to have sex with her boss. In an interview with *People* (10/28/91), she described her early attempts at denial: "Maybe if I work hard and he sees how good I am at my job, he'll leave me alone," she thought.

"You feel powerless," Aleta Carpenter, a former news director of a radio station, testified at a California legislative hearing in 1991. "What did you do to bring it on? You keep digging in your deepest recesses. You think if you did it, there must be something you can do to stop it."

Like many women, Aleta tried to create a sense of control by changing the way she looked. When her boss first started coming on to her, she put her hair in a ponytail and put on her "attitude" glasses, sweat tops, and panty hose "so thick you couldn't see my legs." A top saleswoman who was subjected to advances from several senior managers stopped using makeup and wore fake horn-rimmed glasses. A Milwaukee woman gained more than 20 pounds. "It is probably safe to say that I gained the weight and retain it because it makes me unpalatable to men and I feel safer this way," she wrote.

Other victims blame themselves for not confronting the harasser promptly or at all. Added to the shame of the harassment is the shame of "letting it happen." When Tana's boss started making vulgar comments to her, for example, she said nothing to him. Although she did talk to someone in personnel, "I felt guilt and shame because I didn't have the courage to confront *him* at that time," she testified at a legislative hearing.

No Validation

That so many victims blame themselves isn't surprising. The trauma of sexual harassment has received little recognition in this society.

Until recently, federal law didn't acknowledge that sex discrimination causes emotional injury. The lack of validation makes the experience more painful. One woman described it to 9to5 this way: "Imagine sitting at your desk and seeing a customer walk in bleeding profusely from the head. You try to get your coworkers to notice, but they act as if there is no blood or, if there is, that it's a normal occurrence. Most people ignore your concern. Some laugh at you. A few are irritated. At first you wonder if you're seeing things. You begin to feel crazy. Part of you is angry because you know the blood is real. Another part of you wants to stop worrying, to learn how to fit in. Either way, you feel like a loser."

Other victims have no doubt from the beginning that what's happening is sexual harassment. "I always knew," Aleta Carpenter says. "If someone touches you in places where only you or your husband touch, you know." But these women often have trouble finding anyone else who will see the situation for what it is.

At the radio station where Aleta was a news director, women were commonly referred to as "bitches" in person and on the intercom. One woman with large breasts was told to wear something tighter. "Make sure that your happenings show," the general manager said. After five years on the job, Aleta was terminated because the general manager found her presence "too tempting."

Aleta filed a charge at the EEOC, which did a cursory investigation. Station management wrote to the investigator, saying the general manager hadn't done anything. The EEOC never once came on-site or called anyone in for an interview, even though *more than a dozen women* had been fired for refusing sexual advances at the station. Aleta's case was eventually dismissed.

Humiliation

Humiliation is a word sexual harassment victims commonly use to describe their experience. They feel demeaned and devalued. They go to work to do a job; instead, they're seen as sexual playthings.

Sexual harassment victims also feel embarrassed. Unlike many work-related injuries, this one is difficult to talk about. Virginia called the 9to5 hotline to say that although she'd been harassed several years earlier, she'd been too embarrassed to let anyone know. After the Thomas/Hill hearings, Virginia had told her mother, who revealed that she, too, had been harassed nearly 40 years before and had never told a soul.

"Because sexuality is such a private experience, all forms of sexualized abuse are likely to be deeply humiliating," writes psychologist Jean A. Hamilton, "which creates a conflict between getting help and keeping the secret."*

Loss of Interest in Work

The experience of being harassed can make a job intolerable. Many victims describe the grief they feel when they have to leave a job they love or find themselves unable to enjoy it anymore.

Safer on the Streets Louette Colombano, a former police officer in San Francisco, endured years of extreme physical and verbal sexual harassment. A male officer once reached across the table in a public place and grabbed her breast. On another occasion, she was required to watch while another officer had oral sex with a prostitute. Louette reported these incidents to superiors, but instead of stopping the harassment, they ostracized her. No one would speak to her. Her car was vandalized on a daily basis. Threats were left on her answering machine. One day, she was dispatched to a call involving a man with a gun. She called for backup, but none came.

"I enjoyed my job," Louette testified at sexual harassment hearings in San Diego. "But my childhood dream was turned into a nightmare. I was more comfortable on the street with criminals than I felt inside my own station."

In a Bind

Many victims of sexual harassment find themselves in a bind. If they fight, they risk losing their jobs or the approval of their boss or coworkers. If they *don't* fight, they risk losing their self-respect.

Jump or Burn "I felt like I was standing on the fifteenth floor of a burning building . . . ," a woman who ended up suing her employer told the *Los Angeles Times* (6/28/85). "I had a choice of standing there and being eaten by the flames or jumping out of the window and maybe ending up dead or very injured. I had to jump. I just had to. I could not stay there and be eaten by the flames."

If they reveal their pain, victims may be dismissed as hysterical.

---

*Hamilton, Jean A., Sheryle W. Alagna, Linda S. King, Camille Lloyd, "The Emotional Consequences of Gender-Based Abuse in the Workplace: New Counseling Programs for Sex Discrimination," in *Women and Therapy*, Vol. 6, 1987 (New York: The Haworth Press), p. 165.

The woman is in a difficult situation, writes Dr. Jean A. Hamilton. "Being a victim, she can't afford to act like one. To appear victimized (even hypersensitive or irritable) is risky because it may be taken by crucial decision makers or potential supporters as evidence that the woman is not suffering from discrimination, but that she is really incompetent and deserves whatever she gets." (Hamilton et al., p. 167.) Yet if a victim appears too calm, she still may not be believed. Anita Hill, for example, was not taken seriously by some people because of her steady demeanor at the Senate Judiciary hearings.

Loss of Trust

Sexual harassment undermines trust—in men, in oneself. Carol, for example, has a strong marriage with a supportive husband and two sons. Still, after years of harassment in a warehouse where she was one of only a few women, she feels her heart pounding with fear whenever she passes a group of men standing together.

Three years after she left her job because of harassment, Patrice is still unable to go back to work. "I don't trust myself," she said. "If this happened to me again, I don't know what I might do to someone."

Anger

Victims of severe sexual harassment usually react with rage against their harasser. "I want to go burn [the harasser's] house down," said Lois, the insurance claims adjuster who lost her job when she reported harassment. "I want to hurt him back."

"When I see the guy who harassed me, I just tense up," said another woman. "I wish he would die. For the longest time, when I had no money for food or Christmas presents, I wanted to tell his wife so maybe their marriage would break up and his kid could go without presents, too."

Depression

Anger turned inward ("Why was I so stupid?") or even anger directed at the right target with no constructive outlet can lead to stress and depression. The emotional consequences of harassment can include almost all the symptoms involved in what is known as a "major depressive episode." According to Hamilton and her colleagues,

A major depressive episode is characterized by a dysphoric mood or loss of interest in usual activities or pastimes (e.g., depressed, sad, blue, hopeless, low, down in the dumps, irritable) and at least four of the following present nearly every day for at least two weeks:

- poor appetite or weight loss
- increased or decreased sleep
- loss of interest or pleasure or decreased sexual drive
- loss of energy, fatigue
- feeling of worthlessness, guilt
- decreased concentration
- thoughts of death.

"Sexual harassment really does a number on your self-esteem," Lois says. "I had suicidal thoughts of driving into ditches or off bridges in my company car." Finally, she found herself unable to eat or sleep and checked herself into a mental hospital for five-and-a-half weeks with severe depression. "I still have recurring nightmares," she says—a common response.

Aleta Carpenter testified that she started to drink excessively and then suffered a stress attack. "The kids would say, 'Mom, you're asleep all the time.' It was depression from a sense of powerlessness."

Donna Puckett, a gas-station manager, told *People* magazine (10/28/91) that a supervisor who was visiting from out of town asked her to meet him in his hotel room to discuss a promotion. When she walked in, he was naked. He threw her on the bed and ejaculated on her pants, she says. She filed a complaint—and was then harassed by another company executive. While taking a month-long medical leave, Donna was terminated. "I wouldn't leave the apartment," she said. "I stopped cleaning. I didn't want to talk to my friends or make love with my husband."

Sheila, a black woman who works in a plant with mostly white males, has experienced sexual and racial harassment for years. "They have me crying all the time," she says. "I didn't use to be a crybaby. I've been so depressed, I thought about taking my life. Then I thought, what would my son think? This would harm him. He's the only reason I'm here."

PHYSICAL EFFECTS

It's well known that psychological stress takes a toll on physical health. Those who have experienced severe harassment catalogue a long list of physical symptoms including headaches, backaches, nausea, stomach ailments, fatigue, and sleep and eating disorders. Some women describe having their hair fall out in clumps. Often stress attacks the immune system, lowering the body's resistance to a wide variety of ailments.

- Anna: "I grew tired and anxious, lost sleep, and could not eat. I would throw up in the middle of the night."

- Sally: "I experienced somatic symptoms of extreme distress for the entire two years. I truly do not know how I survived it. . . . I was sick to my stomach that entire time."

- Sheila: "I was under a doctor's care. They had to do a biopsy on my back. He said that I had a condition rare in blacks—that I must be under a lot of stress."

Sexual harassment victims don't always recognize the connection between their physical symptoms and the stress they're experiencing. But sometimes, the physical distress is what finally makes the victim realize she has to take action.

Holly, for example, had advanced rapidly to a management position. Her new boss began pressuring her to stay late and work alone with him in his office. He frequently put his hands on her shoulders and hips and made comments about what a hot lover she must be. Holly tried to convince herself that she could handle the situation. Only after she wound up in the hospital for a stress-related stomach ailment did she decide to talk to the company's affirmative action officer.

ECONOMIC EFFECTS

Undergoing harassment is hard enough emotionally. But many victims suffer economically as well. They lose their jobs and settle for lower-paying ones. They pile up attorney fees and doctor and counseling bills.

Laura's complaint of sexual harassment against her boss was settled out of court. The boss was fired—with severance pay. Laura, who had left the company, took a position at lower pay. After two-

and-a-half years, she's still paying off a large attorney bill. "Victims shouldn't have to go into debt to protect themselves against sexual harassment," she says.

"My son and I have suffered many hardships since the loss of my job," said Deborah, who was fired for refusing to sleep with her boss. "I lost my car, my apartment. I had to sell some of our belongings in order to survive. For a while, we had to go on welfare. Do you know what it's like going shopping at midnight because you can't stand the way the other customers look at you when you pay with food stamps?"

In order to avoid the harasser, victims may avoid situations important to their job duties or career opportunities. And both emotional distress and physical ailments reduce productivity. "I basically stopped functioning," said Jessica, whose machinist job was poisoned by constant physical and verbal sexual harassment. "Sometimes I'd have to repeat an operation four times before I got it right."

If the victim leaves a job because of harassment, she may have a hard time finding another job or feeling safe in it. "Now I have to change fields," said Lois. "I have a huge fear of being in a job interview, being asked why I left. I'm afraid I'll run out of the room. It makes me really angry to think some companies won't consider me if they find out what happened."

Sally was fired from a job because of sexual harassment. At her six-month review at her new job, her manager asked, "What's the matter with you? You act like we're going to walk up and tap you on the shoulder and tell you you're through."

Even those who fight and collect damages say they sustain serious economic losses. "I received less than one year's back wages, much less after my attorney fees were paid," said Betty. "I have been unemployed for almost two years, with no real job prospects, despite an extensive search. My family and I are recovering from the trauma that discrimination caused us to suffer, but our financial situation is devastated."

Melissa, a former police officer, won a sizeable sum from a jury, but the department has appealed the decision and she won't see the money for months or years, if ever. In the meantime, she has had to declare bankruptcy.

In addition to present losses, victims of sexual harassment may experience decreased earnings for a long time to come. Economists have documented the effect of job interruption on a woman's earnings. Leaving a job can mean forfeiting time accrued toward a pension or seniority built up toward a promotion or raise. It can also mean losing health benefits during the very time one might be most in need of medical care. The fact that a significant percentage of women leave their jobs because of harassment also reinforces the stereotype that female workers are not as reliable as men.

EFFECTS ON FAMILY

Family members suffer right along with the harassment victim, experiencing emotional upset as well as financial losses. "The more the woman manages to restrain the anger at work, the more it may spill out at home," says psychiatrist Hamilton (p. 172). A typical harassment victim, says Hamilton, comes home stressed out, yells at the kids or closes herself off emotionally, and then feels guilty for being a lousy mother.

"I was so out of it for the year that the harassment was going on," said Lillian, a legal secretary, "I would go home every night and collapse. It was as if my children had no mother."

Hamilton describes other negative consequences for family members: Women victims may perceive males in the family—like the male harasser at work—as aggressors. They may overreact to roughhousing or a casual comment about a good-looking woman on TV. Daughters may identify with the mother and worry about their own future careers. Husbands can feel angry and powerless (Hamilton et al., p. 173).

"My husband wanted to kill my boss," Lillian remembered. "He couldn't stand to see what I was going through. He felt terrible because there was nothing he could do about it."

EFFECTS ON THE COMPANY

Sexual harassment hurts the company as well as the victim and her family. In 1988, *Working Woman* magazine surveyed 160 large manufacturing and service companies and came up with a startling figure: A typical Fortune 500 company with 23,750 employees loses *$6.7 million a year* because of sexual harassment. And that figure doesn't include lawsuits. What it does include are serious financial losses due to absenteeism, lower productivity, and employee turnover, that is, the costs of rehiring and retraining when talented staff leave because of harassment. Another 1988 study showed that sexual harassment cost the federal government $267 million between 1985 and 1987—$37 million to replace federal workers who left their jobs, $26 million in medical leave due to stress from sexual harassment, and $204 in lost productivity.

Harassment can adversely affect other employees, too, not just the direct victim or victims. Women who fear that they themselves will become the target of unwanted comments or physical contact may go out of their way to avoid interacting with the harasser. As a result, they may slow their own career advancement or reduce their efficiency. In addition, when employees believe the only way to get ahead is to engage in sexual banter or other activity they find offensive, they may suffer the same low morale, lack of trust, and reduced loyalty that the victims themselves are experiencing.

"I have seen situations where entire work groups were utterly destroyed because of sexual harassment," says Gwendolyn Combs, Director of the Nebraska Department of Personnel. "It's difficult to heal those wounds."

After Tana spoke out about the harassment she had experienced, a stream of women employees came by her desk to talk to her. They didn't trust the official grievance procedure because top managers themselves were among those responsible for the offensive behavior. Between the harassment itself and the lack of an effective channel for dealing with it, the women spent hours of work time talking over their frustration and anger. Their lengthy discussions "cost the company many days of productivity," Tana said.

Such costs are measurable. So are the costs of defending or replacing a harasser. But there are other, less calculable losses. Who can measure the damage to a company's reputation and ability to recruit when stories of harassment circulate in the community, especially if they appear in the media? Management might just as well put up a sign announcing, "Talented People: Stay Away."

The cost of a full-scale training program at a Fortune 500 corporation is about $200,000, less than 3 percent of the annual cost of allowing sexual harassment to continue. For smaller companies with fewer resources, the effects of sexual harassment can be even more damaging, and the cost of a training program considerably less, than at a large company.

SURVIVING

Many women who experience harassment prefer to call themselves survivors, not victims. At a legislative hearing in 1992, Kelly testified publicly about her harassment experience. For her, taking action to stop harassment was an important part of the healing process.

After college, Kelly testified, she landed a professional job at a state agency. She was harassed in the direct presence of a top-level manager. Other women supported her privately but told her they'd be afraid to testify on her behalf.

"The situation destroyed me," Kelly testified. "I lost my trust, my confidence, my self-respect, and my career aspirations. My personality drastically changed. I had been happy-go-lucky. I became bitter, withdrawn, and ashamed. I did nothing to ask for or warrant what happened to me. Yet I could not take control, stop it, or solve it."

Six years later, Kelly works at a different state agency. She describes herself as a "successful survivor. No longer does the harassment define how I think of myself. The rage I felt for years and years is no longer there. The bitterness has been replaced by a supportive workplace. But the memories, the sick feeling in my stomach now as I describe the harassment, will always be there. I promised myself I would someday get back at those responsible by telling what happened."

EFFECTS OF SEXUAL HARASSMENT

For Victim	For Company
Denial	Low morale
Self-blame	Reduced loyalty
Humiliation	Damaged reputation
Anger	Absenteeism
Depression	Lower productivity
Weakened immune system	Employee turnover
Sleep or eating disorders	Legal fees
Fatigue	
Headaches, backaches	
Days out of work	
Loss of job	
Attorney fees	
Counseling bills	

5

Why Women Don't Report Sexual Harassment

You don't make an issue of it. You develop one hell of a thick skin.

Dr. Frances Conley, neurosurgeon driven out of her job by 25 years of sexual harassment

Using a pseudonym to protect her privacy, a sexual harassment victim appeared as a guest on a radio talk show. Halfway through the hour, a listener called in to say she'd recognized the guest's voice.

"This woman is one of my closest friends," the caller said. "Until today, I had no idea she'd been sexually harassed." She paused. "And until this moment," she went on, "my friend didn't know that I've been harassed, too. We never talked about it."

The two friends are not unusual. Many victims never tell a soul. Only a handful ever file formal charges or seek any kind of legal help.

• In a 1980 survey in which 42 percent of female federal employees and 15 percent of males claimed they'd been harassed at work, only 2 percent said they'd reported the incidents. (In a 1987 follow-up study, the incidence of harassment remained the same; the number who came forward had risen to a mere 5 percent.)

• A 1988 study of large corporations found that their personnel departments received only 1.4 harassment complaints for every 1,000 female employees.

• An article in *Forbes* magazine (5/15/89) calculated that only 0.0091 percent of the female work force had filed harassment charges at the Equal Employment Opportunity Commission in 1988.

"Ninety-five percent of all women and men who describe sexual harassment fear retaliation and a loss of privacy," says Dr. Mary Rowe, ombudsman on sexual harassment complaints for the Massachusetts Institute of Technology. "They also feel it's pointless to complain—management won't do anything."

Most victims never speak out, and of those who do, many wait years. Why is this so?

IGNORANCE OF THE LAW

Many harassment victims have no idea the offensive behavior is against the law. They figure it just comes with the territory. Among women who called the 9to5 Job Problem Hotline with harassment complaints in 1991, one-third didn't know that sexually explicit pinups, graffiti, and offensive jokes could constitute illegal harassment. Half the callers didn't know that coworkers—not just bosses—could be charged with harassment.

Harassers may be equally ignorant about the illegality of their actions. And to compound the problem, some employers who should know the law are breaking it themselves.

CONFUSION

Many victims of sexual harassment are embarrassed and confused about their experiences. Even when the harassment is undeniable, women may believe that they're overreacting or that their own behavior is to blame. They shouldn't have walked into the boss's office at lunchtime, they decide. Or they shouldn't have made eye contact. And so on.

Victims of other forms of sexual abuse tend to react in the same way. Abused and abuser are usually so closely connected—they're often relatives, neighbors, or family friends—that it can be difficult for the victim to make a clean emotional break. Many victims convince themselves that the abuse isn't important or that the behavior isn't happening at all.

In the same way, it's often difficult for victims to recognize that they're being sexually harassed at the workplace. Sometimes the realization dawns gradually; sometimes suddenly, when the victim loses a job or a promotion. A survey of Fortune 500 companies conducted by *Working Woman* magazine in 1988 found that by the time a woman does come forward, the harassment has generally become very severe—severe enough to warrant firing the offender in 20 percent of all cases.

CONCERN FOR OTHERS

Many women are uncomfortable with conflict. They've been trained to believe it's their job to look out for others, not to fight for their own interests.

"I don't want to hurt my kids," said one woman, explaining why she didn't like speaking to a reporter about her harassment experience. "I don't want them to think of me this way."

"I don't want to hurt *his* wife and kids," said a woman who had decided not to file charges against her harasser.

"The man is my father's best friend," said another. "I don't want to destroy his career."

"We are used to making excuses for men's behavior," wrote Sandra Thompson in the *St. Petersburg Times* (4/4/91). "We're taught to do it from the time we are little girls. 'Your father had a hard day at the office, the factory, the hospital, the courtroom,' we were told, to explain away the kind of behavior by our fathers that we'd never accept from our mothers."

A VARIETY OF FEARS

"They'll say I'm too sensitive."
"They'll say I'm lying."
"They'll say I provoked him."
"They'll think I'm crazy."

As in the case of other kinds of sexual abuse, the main reason victims don't take action is fear—fear of being laughed at, ostracized, vilified, humiliated, or retaliated against by friends, co-workers, bosses, lawyers, judges, and juries.

Fear of Not Being Believed

A harasser sometimes threatens that if the victim reports the incident, he'll deny everything and accuse *her* of approaching *him* sexually. Since severe harassment often occurs without witnesses, the victim fears that her word alone won't be enough.

"This is a case of a nobody going up against a somebody," one woman's boss told her outright. "Don't expect anyone to believe you."

Fear of Humiliation

Reporting sexual harassment can mean describing offensive events repeatedly, in detail, in the presence of company officials, lawyers, agency staff, court personnel—and the harasser himself. To many women, the reporting is fully as embarrassing as the abuse itself.

"It's embarrassing to talk to a stranger when you have to tell what a man said and what they did and what you said and did," Paulette Bartunek Reynolds, an investigator for the Suffolk County (NY) Human Rights Commission, told *Newsday* (10/13/91).

"Victims who choose to complain," writes Catherine A. MacKinnon, a leading sexual harassment theorist, in *Feminism Unmodified* (Harvard University Press, 1987), "know they will have to endure repeated verbalizations of the specific sexual abuse they complain about." For many, "the necessity to repeat over and over the verbal insults, innuendoes, and propositions to which they have been subjected leads them to decide that justice is not worth such indignity."

"Men hardly ever ask sexual favors of women from whom the certain answer is no," conservative activist Phyllis Schlafly testified before the U.S. Senate in 1981. "Virtuous women are seldom accosted by unwelcome sexual propositions or familiarities, obscene talk, or profane language."

Schlafly's assertion supports the common myth that victims who are sexually harassed have somehow encouraged the behavior and, thus, deserve the abuse. Many victims fear that reporting sexual harassment will typecast them as disreputable and make it doubly difficult to be taken seriously on the job.

All too often, the victim's behavior, not the harasser's, becomes the issue. In the courtroom, the judge may allow discussion of the victim's sexual partners, her sexual fantasies, her clothing, her use of sexually oriented language, or her participation in sexual banter.

Appearing before the Senate Judiciary Committee, Anita Hill was accused of being unstable, delusional, schizophrenic, a perjurer, and a spurned woman.

"I have not handled a single case of sexual harassment," says attorney Sarah Burns, former director of the National Organization for Women Legal Defense Fund, "where someone has not alleged that the woman was deluded, was having sexual fantasies, was a lesbian. It's as though [they assume that] a 'normal' woman would not be bothered by sexual harassment."

A Michigan factory worker went to the employee relations manager to complain that coworkers were making obscene remarks and gestures and showing her offensive pictures from *Hustler* magazine. The manager responded by asking her if she'd ever worked as a prostitute. "You feel like you have been 'brain raped,'" she says.

Fear of Ostracism

Evelyn, an accounting clerk in a Georgia electronics firm, tried to stop her supervisor from making lewd comments and reaching under her skirt. When confronting him directly didn't work, she went to a higher official at the company, who did nothing. Finally, she filed a complaint at the EEOC. Once word of her charge got back to the company, her coworkers stopped speaking to her. One morning, she found a skeleton hanging from the ceiling over her desk.

Fear of Damaging a Career or Losing a Job—or Both

Harassment victims also fear losing their jobs or seriously damaging their careers. An office supervisor spoke for many when she told the *Milwaukee Journal*, "I've never come forward and voiced a complaint because I was afraid my career would come to a grinding halt."

Often enough, the only way to report harassment is to lodge a complaint with the harasser himself. Or the harassment victim can find herself taking on an individual who brings so much money or prestige to the institution that management lets him behave as he pleases. "Oh, yes—Mr. So-and-so (or Dr. So-and-so or Professor So-and-so)," the victim will be told. "Of course. Everyone knows about him. But what can we do?"

Keeping Quiet To Save a Career For months, Cathy, a teacher in a rural community, brushed off the sexual advances of her principal, who was also the superintendent of schools in her district. One night at a faculty Christmas party at a colleague's home, she excused herself to go to the bathroom. The principal burst in while she was using the toilet, seated himself on her lap, and urged her once again to have an affair with him. Cathy got him out of the bathroom but never reported the harassment, fearing that she, not he, would wind up out of work if she did.

Harassment for 25 Years Dr. Frances Conley put up with sexual harassment for nearly 25 years before she finally took dramatic action. In June of 1991, she resigned from her posts as chief of neurosurgery at the Stanford Veterans Hospital, tenured professor at the Stanford School of Medicine, and chair of the school's academic senate. In a press conference, she charged that for a quarter of a century, male colleagues had propositioned her, fondled her leg in meetings, commented about the shape of her breasts, and addressed her as "hon" in the operating room.

"The only reason I put up with it for as long as I did is I really wanted to advance," Conley said. "I really wanted to be a neurosurgeon. I thought I could be a good neurosurgeon. Had I made an issue of some of the things that were happening . . . I wouldn't have gotten to where I am."

Conley agreed to return to her job only after the embarrassed Stanford administration promised to get serious about curbing sexual harassment. Specifically, the administration vowed to review whether a man Conley had identified as a leading harasser should remain chair of her department. In February 1992 he was asked to step down.

Conley won her battle, but her story is unusual: few women who quit their jobs over harassment report being coaxed back by their employers. As a result, many women are reluctant to quit a job they worked hard to obtain, or to jeopardize a recommendation that could determine the direction of their career.

UNHEARD VOICES

Even when women *do* speak up, their complaints are sometimes ignored.

Manager Dismisses Complaint

Sandy told her manager that a coworker was bothering her by asking her out again and again, even though she'd said she wasn't interested. He wouldn't stop regaling her with stories about his sex life and boasting to other employees that the two of them were dating. The manager did nothing but advise Sandy to keep quiet about the matter. She quit her job.

Harasser Granted Promotion

Fran Zone worked as an account supervisor at a big advertising agency in Los Angeles. She had a brief affair with a powerful coworker but soon found the situation uncomfortable and decided to end the relationship. To her dismay, the man persisted in pressuring her and other women employees for dates. Zone spoke to a superior, who suggested she dress more conservatively and assured her he would take care of the offending coworker. But the only action he took was to make the coworker a vice president. Zone resigned.

Victim Penalized for "Romance"

Betty, a technician working in a rural doctor's office, wasn't involved in an affair with her harasser—yet management acted as if she were. She'd been on the job for nearly a decade when a manager told her he was in love with her. "He became obsessed with me," she told the *Milwaukee Journal* (12/31/89).

Betty complained to the senior doctor, who took no action. Finally, eight months later, he summoned the two of them and threatened to fire them both if the "romance" didn't stop. "But I came to you eight months ago, and all you did was laugh at me," Betty protested. The doctor replied he had decided to "let the romance run its course."

Betty resigned from the job she'd once loved. "My only fault in this entire episode," she reflects, "was in being naive. I believed that my harasser would realize what he was doing to me and stop. I also believed that my employers would protect me."

Company Psychiatrist Offers No Help

Many victims find therapists who offer them the validation and support they need. Unfortunately, however, there are exceptions.

A physician at a large health facility who was being harassed by a male supervisor sought help from the staff psychiatrist. Although the harassment was severe, she was told simply to pull up her hair, wear glasses, and appear less attractive.

FIRED FOR SPEAKING UP

Some victims are fired for speaking up, while the harassers keep their jobs. Such cases discourage other victims from coming forward to report harassment.

- A woman complained that a coworker sat at his desk masturbating while he watched her work. The woman lost her job, while the man kept his.

- A woman refused to have sex with a hospital administrator and was fired. She later discovered she was at least the fifth woman to lose her job for the same reason. The administrator still works at the hospital.

- A Philadelphia store clerk was raped by a coworker. The boss fired the *woman*; the rapist kept his job.

HIGH PRICE OF LEGAL ACTION

Patricia Swanson told the *Los Angeles Times* (10/16/91) that her boss at a small-town auto dealership would sneak up behind her trying to unhook her bra, put his hand under skirt, grab her between the legs, and follow her into the restroom. After a year of such harassment, he fired her. Swanson took him to court, won the case, and was awarded $1 in damages.

After Swanson received her minuscule settlement, her boss appealed the case, and this time Swanson lost. "In the end, *I* wound up having to pay *his* legal fees," Swanson says. "Every month, I send *him* a check for $50."

Swanson's experience discouraged her and other women in the dealership from taking further action against harassment.

Another Look at Anita Hill

When Anita Hill testified before the Senate Judiciary Committee that Clarence Thomas had harassed her ten years earlier, many people—even many who believed her testimony—wondered why she hadn't reported the harassment when it was happening.

In light of the many obstacles faced by harassment victims, this question is not so difficult to answer. We may never know the whole truth of the Thomas-Hill matter, but one thing is clear: many women who are harassed do exactly what Hill says she did—tell only a few close friends, wind up in the hospital with a stress-related ailment, and suffer for years in silence.

THE IMPORTANCE OF FIGHTING BACK

Many women who do come forward to report sexual harassment agree that for all the difficulties, they're glad they spoke out. Often they feel their actions have benefited other employees, current and future. And they respect themselves for standing up for their rights.

WHY HARASSMENT ISN'T REPORTED

Ignorance of the law

Confusion

Concern for others, including the harasser

Fear of not being believed

Fear of humiliation

Fear of ostracism

Fear of damaging a career or losing a job

6

Sexual Harassment and Men

Most sexual harassment research has focused on women. But it would be a mistake to neglect the male side of the issue. While some men are "hard-core" harassers, the majority are not. Some men are victims of sexual harassment themselves. The relationship between men and sexual harassment merits close attention.

MOST MEN ARE NOT HARASSERS

While most harassers are men, most men are not harassers. Some men offend without meaning to, and others take steps to combat harassment when it occurs in the workplace. Here are three common types of male harassers:

- Hard-core harasser. He chooses to offend women. Fewer than 1 percent of men are "chronic harassers," according to Dr. Barbara Gutek, a psychologist at the University of Arizona business school. (Others put the figure at 5 percent.)
- Macho man. He wears his masculinity on his sleeve. Part of his aim is to impress other men. He behaves most offensively in a group.
- Insensitive man. He has failed to keep up with changes in the work world and objectifies women, thinking of them as workplace adornments. Once he finds out his behavior is offensive, he tries to change it.

Most men genuinely want to avoid harassment and show respect for women. Some are active opponents of sexual harassment. These men don't tell or laugh at jokes that demean women—in fact, they're offended by such humor. They will support or initiate efforts to eliminate offensive behavior at the workplace.

WHY SOME MEN HARASS

If most men are not harassers, why do some men harass women? Until 1964, discrimination against women was legally and socially acceptable in the United States. The impact of hundreds of years of inequality between the sexes can still be felt. Men are socialized to be the initiators of sexual contact—and sometimes to be aggressive about it.

"Many men are accustomed to treating women in rather limited ways," former EEOC chair Eleanor Holmes Norton told *Working Woman* magazine (December 1988), "as sex objects or as relatives, but have little experience in dealing with women as colleagues, peers, workers, or supervisors."

Like other forms of sexual victimization, intentional harassment is not an expression of romantic attraction; it is an exercise of power belonging in the same category of sexual behavior that includes assault and rape. "Sexual harassment is a subtle rape, and rape is more about fear than sex," University of Washington psychologist John Gottman told the *New York Times* (10/22/91).

The linking of sex and violence is widespread throughout society. In 1986, University of California researchers reported that 30 percent of college men said they would commit rape if they could be sure of getting away with it. When the word *rape* was replaced with the phrase *force a woman into having sex,* 58 percent said they'd do so. A survey funded by the National Institute of Mental Health, studying 6,100 undergraduates on 32 college campuses, found that one in four women respondents had had an experience that met the legal definition of *rape* or *attempted rape.*

Women workers are vulnerable not only to sexual harassment but also to other abuses of power, such as discrimination in hiring, promotions, and pay. Harassment *stems from* the power imbalance between men and women at work. It also serves to *perpetuate* that imbalance.

THE SERIOUS HARASSERS: WHO ARE THEY?

Although serious harassers represent only a tiny percentage of men, they're found everywhere—"in all types of occupations, at all organizational levels, among college professors as well as the business and professional world, and among individuals who live otherwise exemplary lives," wrote Dr. Louise Fitzgerald of the University of Illinois in a statement prepared during the Clarence Thomas hearings. "Some harassers are blatant; others are subtle. Some are well known, whereas others may escape detection for years." While most intentional harassers are repeaters, some harass only once in their lives.

Experts have little to say about patterns of harassment. Men who harass women on purpose, they say, tend to be older than their victims, married, and of the same race as their victims. "Sexual harassers tend to take advantage of those whom they perceive as most vulnerable," asserts Rosemarie Tong in *Women, Sex, and the Law* (Rowman and Allanheld, 1984). Because racial stereotyping often has sexual overtones, women of color, who have little power in the workplace as a group, are often targets of harassment.

WOMEN ON MALE TURF

Most harassment cases involve women in traditional occupations—in the clerical, service, and factory jobs where the vast majority of women work. But there's also evidence that women who break into new occupations and work settings become special targets of harassment. In a 1989 study, Los Angeles psychologist Nancy Baker found that women machinists—who held jobs that until recently had been held only by men—reported more harassment than women on the assembly line—a work area integrated years before.

Harassment functioned as an attempt to keep women from infiltrating a male preserve at Texas A&M University. In 1991, of the 1,880 uniformed cadets in the military training program, only 76 were women; and in the elite cadet unit, only 3 out of 50 members were women. When a woman decided to try out for the elite unit, three students brutally assaulted her and threatened her with a knife, she said. Within days of the incident, other women cadets came forward to charge that the campus had a pattern of rapes and beatings and that superior cadets turned a deaf ear.

MEN AS HARASSMENT VICTIMS

For men as a group, sexual harassment is not the same as it is for women. Men are less likely to experience harassment, less likely to suffer if they do, and less likely to live in fear that it will happen. But some men do become victims of sexual harassment. Like women, in some cases they suffer devastating economic and emotional consequences.

It is estimated that 90 percent of sexual harassment cases involve men harassing women, 9 percent involve same-sex harassment, and 1 percent involve women harassing men. In a study released in 1990 concerning Department of Defense employees, 17 percent of male respondents said they'd been harassed (as did 64 percent of females).

Men have won several harassment cases in court. In 1982, a federal judge awarded $25,000 to a Wisconsin state office employee who was demoted after refusing the advances of his female supervisor. In 1991, two male Rhode Island jewelry workers won a case in which they charged that their boss had ordered them to have sex with his secretary.

When men are harassed, in many cases they seem to suffer less severe effects. Harassed women are nine times more likely than men to quit a job, five times more likely to seek a transfer within the same firm, and three times more likely to lose their job involuntarily, according to a 1986 study by Barbara Gutek and A.M. Konrad.

DIFFERENT VIEWS OF HARASSMENT

In general, men and women have different attitudes toward sexual attention at the workplace. Asked what constitutes harassment, men and women agree on many points. But their views tend to differ in some important respects. Dr. Michelle Paludi, a psychologist and coordinator of the Sexual Harassment Panel at New York City's Hunter College, asked men and women to consider the hypothetical example of a department chairman who invites a woman instructor to lunch "to discuss her research." At the restaurant, and at several subsequent lunches, the chairman steers the conversation away from the instructor's work and talks only about her personal life. Later, over dinner and drinks, he tries to fondle her.

Both men and women agreed that the chairman was harassing the instructor. They differed, however, about when the harassment began. "Most of the women said the sexual harassment started at the first lunch, when he talked about her private life instead of her work," Dr. Paludi told the *New York Times* (10/22/91). "Most of the men said that sexual harassment began at the point he fondled her."

American culture allows men to boast about unsolicited sexual attention, while women are more likely to feel ashamed of such contact. In Dr. Barbara Gutek's study of 1,200 employees, 67 percent of men said they would look upon a proposition from a female coworker as a compliment; only 17 percent of women said they'd be flattered by a male coworker's sexual offer.

"In Western society," Gutek says, "men are 'naturally' viewed as serious workers, and a sexual overture or proposition from a woman does not alter that view of them." Confident that he won't be pigeonholed as a sexual object, "a man can relish an overture from an attractive young woman . . . without having to wonder if she will fire him when the affair is over." Of course, there are many exceptions to this broad generalization. Not all men want to be propositioned at work; some female bosses *do* retaliate against males who resist their advances.

Some men who feel flattered by sexual attention on the job can't understand why women feel so offended by it. It's particularly hard for some men to understand why sexual innuendoes, jokes, or posters need to be restricted in the workplace. If a woman isn't being physically harmed or threatened with firing, they wonder, why should she be concerned? And some men can't understand why any woman would suffer harassment in silence.

Although individual men may suffer harassment, women as a group have more reason to fear it. Not only is it more likely to happen to women, it's more likely to cause harm if it does. Women wonder what comes *after* the hand on the shoulder or thigh— physical assault and rape, possibly resulting in pregnancy or AIDS? These dangers are more present for women than for men.

NEW ROLES EVOLVING

As new rules for workplace behavior evolve, some men take the changes in stride. "If you're with the guys, you're going to say one thing," a telephone sales representative told *Newsday* (10/13/91). "If you're with women, you're going to say things differently. Some young ladies you could say a dirty joke to and they wouldn't bat an eye. Some would bat an eye."

But some men are truly confused by the changing times. "Unless you just keep your mouth shut," one man complained, "you're bound to make a remark that offends someone. Touch a woman's shoulder and you could be hauled into court."

In a work world controlled by men, women have traditionally had to adjust to male expectations if they want to keep their jobs. Now men find that they are expected to modify their behavior to meet women's needs. While many find that the new rules aren't as arbitrary or complicated as they feared, others have difficulty accepting them. "I had a man tell me he wasn't going to talk to any more female employees because he was so shell-shocked," one sexual harassment trainer told *Newsday* (10/13/91) after a session at a Long Island, New York, workplace.

HOW NOT TO HARASS: SOME GUIDELINES

Men who seek to avoid offending women on the job can follow these guidelines:

- Until you learn otherwise, assume that a woman you don't know will *not* enjoy off-color jokes or sexual advances at work.

- Sharpen your listening skills. If a woman's response, whether verbal or physical, seems negative, trust that it is. Does she avert her eyes or turn away? Assume that no means no.

- If you're not sure whether your workplace behavior is acceptable, ask yourself how you'd feel if your wife, daughter, or sister were witnessing your words and actions or were on the receiving end of such behavior.

Men who decide they *have* offended a coworker can consider discussing the matter directly: "I'm afraid our conversation made you uncomfortable the other day. Is this true?" Take the woman's response seriously and assure her you'll try not to offend her again.

TAKING A STAND AGAINST HARASSMENT

Individual men can do a great deal to curb offensive behavior on the job. And such action is important. While laws and official company policies can provide a useful framework for combating sexual harassment, what truly counts is how employees are treated at the workplace day to day.

Men can speak up when they see other men harassing a female employee. They can refrain from telling or encouraging jokes that demean women, whether among male or female colleagues.

If you witness harassment, whether you're a man or a woman, offer your support to the victim. Make it clear that the victim is right to be offended and that the harassment also offends *you*. If possible, offer to speak to the harasser. But follow the lead of the person who's been harassed; offer suggestions rather than pursuing a path the victim isn't ready for. Press management (and your union, if you have one) to provide education about harassment and to adopt an effective complaint procedure.

SEXUAL HARASSMENT AND MEN

Most harassers are men, but most men are not harassers.

Intentional harassment is an exercise of power, not romantic attraction.

Harassment happens in every kind of occupation, every industry.

Ninety percent of harassment cases involve men harassing women. Nine percent involve same-sex harassment. One percent involve women harassing men.

In general, men and women have different views of what constitutes harassment.

7

What to Do if It
Happens To You

---

*A department head circulated a cartoon featuring a scantily clad
woman sitting on a man's lap. "Just what I wanted," the caption read.
"A laptop." One employee routed the cartoon back to the sender—with
a copy of the company's sexual harassment policy attached.*

---

*When women first started working at a steel plant, male workers
would howl like dogs every time the women entered the room. One
woman bought a box of dog biscuits to toss at the men as needed.*

Maybe you've been experiencing sexual harassment in one form or
another for years. Maybe you're experiencing it now for the first
time. Or perhaps something at work is making you uncomfortable,
and you're not sure whether to call it harassment or not. What
should you do?

TRUST YOUR INSTINCTS

When social workers teach children about sexual assault and
unwanted touching, they talk about the "uh-oh" feeling. You don't
have to have a big vocabulary or lots of experience to understand
that. If something makes you feel that way, the children learn, you
don't have to take it. You should tell someone you trust right away.

That doesn't mean every questionable comment or gesture signals serious sexual harassment. You may want to see if it happens again or check in with someone else. But if the "uh-oh" feeling gets triggered, don't ignore it.

The Not-So-Invisible Man

"Don was always breathing on me," Louise said. "He would call me into his office and shut the door. I was really uncomfortable. He was always bumping into my chair and rubbing my arm. The more he did that, the worse I felt. Once in the copy room, he brushed up against me with his whole body; then he stepped back and did it again. Finally, I realized I was not imagining any of it."

Get Emotional Support

Talk to someone you feel comfortable with—maybe a coworker or a friend outside of work. If you're in a union, talk to your steward or someone on the women's committee, if any. (See Chapter 12 for more on this.) You may also want to call a local advocacy organization or counseling center.

You may need to hear that sexual harassment is not your fault and not a figment of your imagination. Victims of sexual harassment also need a safe place to express anger. (The anger is understandable and legitimate, but yelling at the harasser at work may be risky.) And you need basic information on your rights and your options for action.

Gaining Confidence

Bonnie, a skilled machine operator, was being harassed by her boss. One day he rubbed his arm against her breast and asked, "What color are your pubic hairs?" Bonnie left work crying. She left a message with the personnel office and then called the 9to5 hotline.

"The 9to5 counselor gave me the support I needed and the confidence to talk to personnel," Bonnie said. "She helped me realize I was not at fault." When someone from personnel called her back, Bonnie was ready. She gave a detailed account of the harassment. The next day the personnel manager met with the harasser, who acknowledged that he had made the offensive comments and gestures. He received a severe warning and hasn't bothered Bonnie again.

SAY NO CLEARLY

Saying no immediately and clearly is often enough to make the harasser stop the offensive behavior. If a verbal no does *not* stop the behavior, or if you feel uncomfortable with a verbal no, say no in writing. Try to deliver your written no in person and with a witness. You don't need to send a copy to anyone besides the harasser at first, but keep a copy of the memo in your personal files away from the office. If you file a charge later on, the harasser may say that he had no idea you were uncomfortable with his behavior. Your letter will thwart that defense.

Say no, either verbally or in writing, in any tone that feels right to you. Here are some samples:

"It makes me uncomfortable when you talk to me/touch me/look at me that way. I'm not questioning your intentions, but I would prefer that you not do it again. I hope we can have a good professional relationship."

"As I have indicated on numerous occasions, I am not interested in going out with you. Your requests for dates are making me uncomfortable. If you continue, I will have to bring the matter to the attention of someone higher up."

"I don't appreciate your brushing up against my body. You know that these incidents are not accidental. If you don't act in a professional way, I will report this harassment."

"If you touch me/talk to me that way one more time, I'll report you so fast you won't know what hit you."

"Why don't we step into the outer office so you can make that request in front of the rest of the staff?"

"Do you think top management would appreciate having to deal with a lawsuit brought on by your behavior?"

"Sure, I can take a joke. What I won't take is sexual harassment. If you don't know the difference, I'll be glad to recommend some reading material."

Many sexual harassment victims blame themselves for giving the wrong message by not saying no strongly enough. But saying no directly isn't always easy, especially if the harasser is your boss. And most people who are sexually harassed communicate their discomfort in dozens of ways—by not saying yes or thanks, by not smiling, by stiffening up or looking perturbed. Chances are that the harasser gets the message; in fact, your discomfort may be just what he was looking for. It's not that he doesn't know what bothers you, he simply thinks he can get away with it.

Setting Him Straight

Michelle, a plumber, sought counseling from a women's group after her first experience with sexual harassment. The second time, when Norman, another plumber, began to pressure her for dates and squeeze up against her, she acted promptly. In front of the boss, she talked to Norman explicitly about the behavior and named those who had witnessed it. "If it happens again," she told him, "I'm taking you to court." Norman never bothered her again.

Putting It in Writing

If you decide to put your no in writing, Mary Rowe, special assistant to the president of the Massachusetts Institute of Technology, recommends that the letter have three parts: first, a detailed, objective account of the offensive behavior; then a description of how that behavior made you feel; and finally a statement of what you want to happen next. Here is a sample:

"Every Monday morning for the past four weeks you've stopped at my desk to tell me about your sexual exploits over the weekend. I am very embarrassed by these comments. It's hard for me to get back to my work, and I find myself trying to avoid having to see you. I want you to stop making these remarks to me."

DOCUMENT EVERY INCIDENT IN DETAIL

Many people do say no and find that it gets them nowhere. They may even report the harassment and get no support from management. The former EEO officer at one woman's company told her, "Keep your mouth shut and take the shit. It will get better." Keeping a log makes it easier to get results from top management or government agencies. Include the date, time, location, and a description of each incident of harassment, with accurate detail about what was said or done. Some women have the log notarized to verify the time period. Use a bound notebook to which sheets of paper can't be added. You can also mail a copy of your documentation to yourself and keep it in the postmarked, sealed envelope.

The log is not so much to refresh your own memory as to give legitimacy to your complaints if you choose to report them to management. Many women who call the 9to5 hotline have an amazing ability to recall events that happened up to 50 years earlier. As one woman told the Senate Judiciary Committee, "I didn't need to write it down. I remembered every place on my body this man touched me." Still, Anita Hill's testimony was dismissed by many senators for lack of documentation.

DOCUMENT YOUR JOB PERFORMANCE

Keep copies of your job evaluations and any memos that attest to the quality of your work. If you receive verbal praise, write a note of thanks to create a record of it ("Thanks for telling me how impressed you were with the Jones report.") Again, keep these *away from the office*, just in case someone tampers with your files. The harasser might try to defend himself by going on the offensive: "She was a poor performer and just wanted to get back at me for not giving her a promotion."

Not Prepared

Lois's boss subjected her and other staff to displays of pornographic materials and embarrassing comments. Eventually, Lois was contacted by this man's superior, who had gotten complaints from other women in the office. Lois corroborated their stories. Her boss received a mild reprimand.

After that, although Lois's performance had been excellent, her boss began to criticize everything she did. "I started getting huge red notes on my desk, saying 'You're not returning your phone calls. You have to do a better job,'" Lois said. Her boss gave her a low rating on her performance review so she wouldn't get a raise. Because she never anticipated the retaliation, Lois wasn't prepared with documentation.

Armed and Ready

Hannah's boss repeatedly pressured her to have sex with him. If she reported him, he warned, he would say she was just trying to cover up her poor performance. But Hannah had strong documentation of her good work. Her evaluations were all above average. She had letters from three managers complimenting her work and a special commendation she'd received for completing a difficult project ahead of schedule. Hannah did report the harassment, and her boss was demoted.

LOOK FOR WITNESSES AND OTHER EVIDENCE

Sexual harassers are often (although not always) repeat offenders. Start by asking coworkers and former employees, both women or men, whom you know and trust. You might want to check with other women who deal with the harasser. If you can get a group of women to complain collectively, it will be much harder for the company to ignore the behavior or to protect the harasser.

I Won't Go Quietly

Anna worked as a staff engineer for an environmental engineering firm. After three months, she received a $3,000 raise. Then, the night before her six-month review, Harvey—Anna's boss and the sole owner of the firm—came to her apartment at 11:30 P.M. Thinking he must be having car trouble, Anna let him in. Instead, Harvey claimed it was his wife he was having trouble with. Soon it became clear what kind of help Harvey wanted. Anna finally got him to leave, but not before he had opened his overcoat and lunged at her with an animalistic roar.

The next morning, Harvey told Anna that he had made a big mistake and that it would never happen again. Things were fine for about a month. Her review went well, her work was commended, and she received another raise. Then Harvey began criticizing her work. He barked orders and never had time to answer questions about her projects. Anna realized her work was being distributed to the other engineers.

Anna confided in a male coworker, who suggested she look into why some of the women before her had left the company. Anna found out she was not alone. Four of the women she reached had had a problem with Harvey's advances. Two told stories almost identical to hers.

Anna confronted Harvey. She told him she knew about the other women. If he did not change his attitude and allow her to do her job, she said, she would not leave quietly, as the others had; she'd sue. Soon after, Anna's projects were restored to her.

Don't Assume You're Alone

It may be difficult to find support. You may be the only woman in your work area. Or the women with whom you work may have gotten the message that going along with offensive behavior is the easiest way to survive on the job. It's best not to judge women who haven't spoken up. They may be more willing to come forward if they feel you're on their side, not pointing a finger at them.

Dana was one of three women working at a brokerage firm. When the dozen men in the department made crude, sexist remarks, Dana would object while the other female brokers kept quiet. "They've all sold out," she thought. Then one day in the women's room, Dana overheard another broker crying. "If that guy puts his hands on my leg one more time," she said, "I swear I'll break his fingers. But then I'll be the one who gets fired." Dana realized she had mistaken fear for indifference. The three women met outside of work and planned how to bring their concerns to the president of the company.

RESEARCH AND USE COMPANY AND UNION CHANNELS

If the harassment continues, find a sympathetic manager. Your company may have designated particular people as those to receive complaints about harassment; or it may be up to you to figure out who in managment can help solve the problem. Use your support system to practice what you'll say. After your conversation, send a memo such as this: "Thank you for meeting with me May 28 on my concerns about sexual harassment in the Purchasing Department. You said you would immediately start an investigation and that I should hear something no later than June 15. I understand that everything I told you will be kept confidential and that you will check to make sure there is no retaliation taken against me." Check in if no one gets back to you.

Utilizing company channels doesn't always bring results. But many women feel they're reclaiming their integrity by making formal complaints. Sheila, who has fought harassment for years in her predominantly white and male department, put it this way: "They thought I was nobody, just a black woman. But I'm somebody. They can't take that away."

Read It and Weep

If you feel uncomfortable about having to describe the harassment out loud, try writing it down.

While on a business trip, Kendra's colleague subjected her and other female executives to vulgar jokes. "Leave your door unlocked," he told her. "I'll be there with only my socks on." Kendra made sure she was never alone with this man. After the trip, she and another woman reported him to his superior but weren't sure they wanted to go through with the investigation; they were afraid they would have to repeat the sexual remarks. They were advised by 9to5 to write the comments down on paper instead, which they did. The investigation resulted in the harasser's being transferred to another city and in sexual harassment training for all employees.

Afraid To Speak Up

Sometimes it's difficult to use company channels because you fear that you will not be protected or that your career will suffer.

Claudia was a high-level manager at a Fortune 500 company. Earl, the vice-president in charge of her division, often grabbed her arms and held her tightly against her will. One day, Claudia and Earl met with her immediate supervisor to discuss her job description. "You don't need a job description," Earl told her, "you need a good fuck." Her supervisor said nothing.

"Corporate officers in these companies are like gods," Claudia says. "No one wants to challenge them." She felt violated by Earl, but she also felt it would be career suicide to file a charge against him. She left the firm and went to work at a rival company.

Today, Claudia feels she would have handled the situation differently. "I would have recognized what was going on earlier and confronted him directly," she says. "Then, if the harassment had continued, I would have gone to his superior."

In fact, informing management about harassment is not a hostile act—it's actually in the best interests of the company. When reporting harassment, you may want to remind management that your actions will benefit the organization. Say that the firm will be hurt by allowing such behavior to continue and that you feel an obligation to speak up so that the harasser will stop before he can cause any more damage. Point out that employees who suffer in silence are less likely to work at peak performance and that those who quit represent a loss of talent and a wasted investment in training. The victim who leaves may also file a lawsuit that exposes the company to expensive legal fees and bad publicity.

In companies with an effective policy, employees speak up quickly, get prompt relief, see the harassment end, and feel empowered.

When the System Works

Martha worked as a housekeeper for the Omaha Housing Authority. The agency had a strong sexual harassment policy, including written procedures, constant reminders, and open discussions with employees. When Martha was harassed by a male coworker, she felt confident in the process and reported the incident right away. Martha requested that she and her coworker meet with a person in Human Resources. The coworker admitted his misconduct, apologized, and received a written reprimand. Martha was told she could choose to transfer or have her coworker transferred, but she felt they would be able to work together without a problem.

QUIT IF YOU HAVE TO

In some circumstances, harassment is so severe and channels for remedy within the company so inadequate that the best way to protect yourself is to leave the company. In this case, arrange for a good *written* reference (and unemployment compensation) before leaving the job. Attach the reference to your resume.

Legally, a company is not permitted to give you a bad reference if you leave because of sexual harassment. But your boss may refuse to give you something suitable in writing. Some women in these circumstances have an acquaintance at another firm call for a reference in order to check what the former employer is saying.

If you leave a company as a result of sexual harassment, what do you say in interviews for a new job? When asked why you left your last job, should you tell the truth? In many cases, the best approach is to say simply that you left to find a better fit for your experience and interests. Emphasize that you are looking for a job that will be stable and long-term.

If you decide to tell your prospective employer the truth, be brief. Don't offer details or negative comments about the company you left. Even if the interviewer expresses interest in what happened, say little and move on. One of these comments may be sufficient:

- "Unfortunately, I experienced sexual harassment and was unable to get the behavior to stop. I want to work at a company where I can utilize my skills and develop my potential without having to worry about this kind of treatment."

- "I understand this company has a strong policy against sexual harassment. My previous job did not, and I preferred not to stay there."

- "I am impressed with this company's commitment to its female employees. That was not true on my last job."

FILE A CHARGE WITH THE STATE OR FEDERAL ANTIDISCRIMINATION AGENCY

If company channels don't exist or don't work, go to a government agency. You have this option even if you are also pursuing company channels.(See Chapter 11 for details.)

CONSIDER CONSULTING AN ATTORNEY

If your company has a strong policy against sexual harassment and moves quickly and sensitively to stop it or if you feel reasonably certain that what you need is to consult the EEOC or other fair employment agency, you don't need a lawyer. But if top management is not responsive or if you aren't ready to approach an agency, then speaking to a lawyer can be helpful. Ask for a referral from the local Bar Association (the professional organization for attorneys) or from a woman's group, civil rights organization, or rape crisis center or other agency that deals with sexual assault.

Make sure the lawyer you speak to specializes in employment discrimination and has a track record of representing the *plaintiff* (the person bringing the charge against the company). The lawyer who drew up your will or helped you buy property may not be the best one to represent you in this situation.

Some attorneys offer a free consultation in which they give you an assessment of your case. (In a number of cities, 9to5 works with cooperating attorneys; all 9to5 members are entitled to a free legal consultation.) Ask for an estimate of the total cost. Is there a printed fee schedule? a sliding scale? Get a clear idea of the expected payment plan and how you will be kept informed of any additional costs that may arise. Some attorneys may be willing to take your case on a contingency basis (you pay only if you win). Or the lawyer may be willing to handle your case without charge (*pro bono*). Damages in most sexual harassment cases are likely to be small or nonexistent, however, so many attorneys will want money up front or may be unwilling to take your case at all.

Look for a lawyer who can demystify the legal process by informing you of what to expect at every stage—sometimes by roleplaying. Even if there is no satisfactory legal remedy for your situation, a lawyer should help simply by stressing that what happened is wrong and just cause for anger and pain. Lawyers should make referrals to local resources—such as advocacy groups, free or low-cost counseling, therapists, and support groups.

You can check with the Board of Attorneys' Professional Responsibility to see if an attorney has ever been disciplined (call the local Bar Association). If you are out of work, the local Legal Services office may assign you an attorney.

GET OUTSIDE SUPPORT

In some cases, the best tactic may be to take your case to the media or to get support from an advocacy group that will give you extra clout. Victims who call on 9to5, for example, often benefit from having an outside group on their side.

Help From Outside Stops Harassment

Denise worked at night cleaning offices with her male supervisor. Whenever she came near him, he would put out his arm and block her way so he could rub up against her body. Denise was afraid that if the harassment went on much longer, "I'd slug the guy and be arrested for battery." She came to the 9to5 office for advice.

A few weeks later, Denise came back. "I told the guy that everything he had ever done to me was now documented with a working women's organization," she said. "He never touched me again."

Raising Consciousness

Noreen was sexually harassed by the manager of the convenience store where she worked. When she complained to the owner, he told her she brought the harassment on herself by the way she dressed. Noreen's mother called 9to5, and a staffperson met with Noreen and her coworkers. These employees backed up Noreen's story, saying the manager harassed them, too, and even bothered customers. They took 9to5 handouts on sexual harassment and put them under the owner's office door. Two days later, the manager was fired. The owner sent a message to 9to5, thanking the organization for the information. "I really appreciated that," he said. "I just didn't understand before."

LET PEOPLE KNOW HARASSMENT CAUSES STRESS

If you seek medical treatment or unemployment benefits, mention the harassment. A doctor who treats any symptoms that may be related to stress should know about the incidents of harassment. If you feel forced to leave your job and file for unemployment, write down "sexual harassment" as the reason you left. This will be useful in documenting your case.

FIND A WAY TO SPEAK OUT

Even if it's not possible for you to take action at the time or if too much time has already passed, there are things you can do:

- Tell your story to someone who will understand—a friend, your sister, your mother—or call the 9to5 hotline. This organization often receives calls from women who experienced sexual harassment years earlier. In many cases, they've never told anyone else what happened. After calling the hotline, many also go on to call their elected officials to press for stronger harassment laws.
- Join a support group if one exists in your city. (See Chapter 8.)
- Get involved in lobbying. Many states have bills pending to strengthen the laws against harassment. Personal testimony from those who have experienced harassment is critical for winning legislative support. Never underestimate the value of your own story, told in your own words.

"I had many sleepless nights before I decided to testify," Tana told legislators at a hearing on sexual harassment. "But what they did was wrong and you need to know about it. I thought about my favorite quote from Eleanor Roosevelt: 'I gain strength, courage, and confidence by every experience by which I must stop and look fear in the face. . . . We must do the things we fear we cannot do.'"

- Write a letter to the editor of your local newspaper telling what happened and urging readers to do what they can to combat sexual harassment. Request anonymity if you wish.
- Join a local women's organization. Even if you don't get actively involved, your dues will help pay for counseling and for materials on sexual harassment, and membership numbers count with policymakers.
- Get together with other women to brainstorm about how to get a sexual harassment policy adopted at your workplace. (See Chapter 13.)
- If appropriate action isn't taken when a public official is found guilty of harassment, speak up! Women's groups in Wisconsin launched a campaign against the awarding of a $39,000 contract to Richard Matty, the former Tourism

Director who had left office after harassing his secretary and placing an article about the state in a Japanese "girlie" magazine. As public criticism mounted, Matty resigned.

DON'T BLAME YOURSELF

No matter what the outcome of your situation, you are not at fault. The overwhelming majority of harassment victims have chosen not to come forward because they felt the risks outweighed the benefits. Their fears were understandable. What's needed is to minimize the risks and maximize the benefits—not to blame the victims.

Dealing with harassment is a process of regaining control after the harasser sought to take it away from you. How you do that will vary depending on your circumstances. It may mean getting far away from the situation. It may mean fighting back. It's important to see your response as something *you* choose out of the options available to you. But it's also helpful to remember this: many women have not taken action against sexual harassment for fear they would be fired—and wound up being fired anyway. Sometimes the *best* protection is to speak up.

Making a choice can be empowering in and of itself. You who have been the *object* of someone's behavior can turn yourself into a *subject* in your own right.

WHAT TO DO IF IT HAPPENS TO YOU

Trust your instincts.

Get emotional support.

Say no clearly.

Document every incident in detail.

Look for witnesses and other evidence from coworkers or former employees.

Research company and union channels and use them.

File a charge with a local, state or federal antidiscrimination agency if necessary.

8

Getting and Giving Support

For anyone who's being sexually harassed, the most important need is for the harassment to stop. If the victim has been fired, she may need back pay or her job back. But most people who have experienced long-term harassment—or even one or two particularly offensive episodes—also have an important immediate need for support.

GETTING SUPPORT

If you've been harassed, you need people who can help you see that what happened to you was wrong and that what you're feeling is normal.

Seek Out Someone Who Understands

You may have a friend who's had a similar experience. Maybe you remember talking to someone during the Clarence Thomas hearings who was especially concerned about the effect of sexual harassment on the victim. If you're in a union, talk to someone on the women's committee or the sexual harassment committee, if there is one. Call a local advocacy or counseling group, a rape crisis center, or the 9to5 Job Problem Hotline. See if there's a sexual harassment support group in your area. You need to talk to people who know what you've been through and who can listen without judging or questioning your responses.

Consider Seeing a Professional Counselor

Many victims of sexual harassment seek help from a professional therapist. Some find this useful even if the harassment occurred long ago. You may want to be "strong" and get on with your life, but don't underestimate the need for a recovery process, a time to mourn and to heal.

Look for Support from Coworkers

Some may hesitate to get involved. But others, both women and men, will be able to give personal support that will be especially valuable during the work day. And some will give even more.

Actions Speak Louder than Words   Linda, a security guard at a college, was being sexually harassed by a supervisor. Her coworker, James, was angry that the administration wasn't doing anything about the offensive behavior. He called 9to5 for a brochure on sexual harassment and delivered it to a manager.

Be Realistic About How Relatives and Friends Will React

Don't be surprised if the people you usually count on for support—immediate family members and close friends—are of little help in this situation. Remember how you felt about harassment before it happened to you. You might not have appreciated how serious harassment can be. Don't set yourself up for disappointment by expecting understanding from family members who may not be able to provide it.

Lois was hospitalized for five weeks after being harassed by her boss. "When I got out of the hospital, I called my father and said, 'Dad, I just spent five weeks in the hospital for depression.' He said, 'Everyone gets depressed now and then.'"

"When I told my parents what happened, my father blamed me," said another sexual harassment victim. "My mother blamed herself."

Deborah's family was sympathetic, but they couldn't understand what she was going through. "They expect me to be all better already," she said.

Be explicit about what you need. If you want to let off steam, let your friends and family know that. If you want advice, ask for it. Naming what you *don't* want can help, too: "I'm afraid you'll blame me in some way. Even if you don't completely agree with my perspective, I just need you to listen and give me a hug."

If you know a particular family member is likely to give you a hard time, avoid talking about the harassment with that person for now. Give yourself permission to pick and choose what you say and to whom. But you may also find that telling your story will change some family members' view of sexual harassment. Gina, for example, was watching the Clarence Thomas hearings on TV with her parents. Her father didn't believe Anita Hill and kept muttering what nonsense her story was. Gina burst into tears. "It's happening to me right now, Dad," she said. "I was afraid to tell anyone." Her father was sympathetic.

The Men in Your Life   Some women hesitate to tell their husband or boyfriend about the harassment for fear he'll want to deal aggressively with the harasser. Try stating your fear and explaining what you want: "I'm afraid you'll want to go down there and beat him up. Sometimes I wish you would. But I know I have to handle this through company channels/through a lawsuit/face to face." Your husband or boyfriend can help you decide what to do, roleplay what you'll say, accompany you to meetings with an attorney or the EEOC, help you review your documents.

Many women find that talking to a husband or boyfriend about a past experience with harassment strengthens their relationship. For example, Dorothy's husband was angry after she quit a good job and the family suffered financial consequences. During the Clarence Thomas hearings, she said to her husband, "Remember that job I quit? That's why—the same thing happened to me that happened to Anita Hill." Her husband was shocked and regretful. A major bone of contention in their marriage disappeared.

Don't Accept Blame

It's natural to doubt yourself ("Why was I so naive?" "Why didn't I do something about it sooner?"). But remember that your experience with harassment is part of the overall problem of sex discrimination. Putting your experience in a larger context will help get you through the criticism that others—the harasser, a manager, a coworker, a friend, a family member, or a U.S. senator—may direct at the harassment victim either explicitly or implicitly. The statements minimizing sexual harassment run the gamut, and every one of them blames the victim:

- Nothing happened (you're a liar/you're delusional/you've got a crush on him).

- It was a joke (you're a bad sport/you aren't ready for the big time).
- It was no big deal (you're overly sensitive).
- It could have been nipped in the bud (you're a wimp for not saying no).
- He got the wrong signals (you're a tramp).
- He's an asset to the company; he has a family to provide for (you're a snitch/you're a troublemaker).

Remember: sexual harassment is not the fault of the victim. You have a right to work in a harassment-free environment. Blaming the victim only lets the harasser and his employer off the hook.

Give Yourself Credit

Recognize the strength you've used to make it through your experience. And take pride in your progress. One woman told 9to5:

"I'm not afraid anymore. They count on you being afraid so you won't be able to proceed. The hardest thing is to keep telling yourself you didn't deserve this and that it's the right thing to pursue it. Once I got a handle on the fear element, I got a lot better.

"It's hard not to be bitter. But in some ways what happened is turning out to be a blessing. I have a better sense of who I am, what's really important to me. I have friends from the support group I didn't have six months ago. I'm happier than I have been for the last five years. I'm not there yet. But I have a sense of inner peace. I feel stronger."

GIVING SUPPORT

If a victim of sexual harassment comes to you for support, consider what she needs:

• **Validation.** What is happening or has happened is harassment and not her fault. Keep reminding her that harassment is discrimination, that it's against the law, and that it has happened to millions of women. Even if she wishes she had done things differently, remind her that nothing that she did or didn't do excuses the harasser.

• **Affirmation.** How she feels is legitimate and normal, even if you don't completely understand it. Make statements like "I can see this really hurts" rather than questioning why she feels that way.

- **Listening without judging.** You might think you would have handled the situation differently. That's irrelevant. The last thing a person who's experienced harassment needs is to hear, "I would never have stood for that." Offer an ear and a shoulder, and keep your judgments to yourself.

- **Flexibility.** Sometimes the victim needs to talk about what happened; other times she may want to focus on anything but. Take your cue from her and give her room to do either. Invite her to go out and get away from the pressure. But don't make her feel guilty for needing to talk about the harassment when she does.

- **A safe place to get angry.** Some of her anger may be displaced onto you or others she's close to. Acknowledging her need to express anger about the situation may help her find appropriate outlets.

- **Referral to experts.** The person who experiences sexual harassment may need some things you can't give. She may need to see a therapist or a lawyer or to meet with others who've been harassed. You can research what resources are available in your area and encourage her to make use of them. Local agencies or hospitals dealing with sexual assault should be able to make referrals to therapists who specialize in cases involving violence against women.

- **Reassurance.** Let her know that there are people who care and that things can get better.

FORMING A SUPPORT GROUP

Some women have formed support groups where individuals who've experienced sexual harassment can discuss their feelings and exchange useful information. The purpose is to "open doors to victims, women who seek a bond to hold on to, to trust, to feel that they are okay and they are not alone," says Linda Moore, the founder of 9to5's support group in Milwaukee. "The group can't undo all the psychological damage of severe harassment," Moore says. "But with support, a healing process can take place much quicker than when you are isolated and alone."

It's not difficult to form a group. First, you need to find some other women who've experienced harassment. It's easiest to do this through the help of a women's group or hotline, but you may also be able to get names through lawyers or therapists who specialize in such cases. Then you need to find a place to meet. If someone's home isn't available, a church or local community group may be willing to provide free space.

In some cases, the group, including the facilitators, consists entirely of victims. Other groups are led by volunteer therapists. Here are some guidelines:

- The support group need not provide therapy. Rather, it can be a place to share stories and information in an informal environment.

- Membership in the group should be free of charge. (Some professional therapists use support groups as part of their treatment; in that case, they charge a fee.) Members can decide how often to meet—weekly, bi-weekly, or monthly.

- Members come to share feelings and experiences, not to give advice or pass judgment. Ground rules for the group should encourage people to use "I" statements ("I want to talk about . . ." rather than "We should talk about . . ."). Members should speak directly to one another ("Mary, you sound angry to me" rather than "Mary sounds angry").

- Members can encourage each other to avoid blaming themselves. ("You call yourself stupid for not having spoken up earlier. Would you say the same thing about another woman in the group?")

- Confidentiality is essential. No one should repeat or discuss anything said in the group without permission.

- Everyone should have the opportunity to share. If one person feels particularly needy, she may ask the group for extra time, but no one should dominate. Members also have the right to remain silent.

- Members should try to avoid interrupting and should give supportive attention to the person speaking.

- The group may work better with a trained facilitator. If several members want to share the role of facilitating meetings, they can look for training from a local counseling center.

Because sexual harassment can be so difficult to handle, group members often need support between meetings as well. The group can set up a buddy system for those who want to call each other or get together between meetings. (Sometimes well-meaning facilitators try to be available to every member. This is a sure-fire road to burnout.)

Some people will be ready to leave the group after a while. They may want to get away from the issue of sexual harassment and get on with other areas of their life. Others may decide that the best way to heal is to stay involved in helping to empower others. There's no "right" choice.

Victims don't merely want to *survive* bad treatment; they want to *end* it. While support is important, so is justice. In the final analysis, the real solution for victims of sexual harassment lies in changing corporate policies, strengthening laws and the legal system, and creating equality in the workplace.

GETTING SUPPORT FOR YOURSELF

Seek out someone who understands.

Consider seeing a professional counselor.

Look for support from coworkers.

Be realistic about how relatives and friends will react.

Give yourself credit.

GIVING SUPPORT TO A VICTIM

Validate that harassment is wrong.

Affirm her feelings.

Listen without judgment.

Refer to experts for help.

9

What Every Good Manager Should Do

Carla told her supervisor that Tim kept massaging her neck and upper back. The supervisor responded, "Is he any good?"

Make managers and supervisors directly responsible. This forces them to be more aware of the problem and to do something about it.

Fred Baxley, EEO Coordinator, Texas Industries, Inc.

Preventing and dealing with sexual harassment takes more than a good policy on paper. Managers need to know how to spot problems and encourage victims to speak up. Equally important, they need to know how to promote the policy as a matter not of rules but of respect. The manager's role is key in setting a tone of mutual consideration, not humorless repression.

WHAT SHOULD A GOOD MANAGER DO?

- Be a role model. Managers who don't make or laugh at remarks that demean women have more credibility in combating sexual harassment. Be mindful of the power imbalance between you and your staff. Avoid even the appearance of improper conduct.

- Be a good listener. Employees are more likely to discuss concerns about harassment with a manager who makes time for them on a regular basis.
- Be nonjudgmental. Label behavior, not people. Don't reprimand someone in front of other staff, and don't gossip.
- Be objective and consistent. Managers have to be willing to acknowledge their own prejudices.
- Be tuned in. If someone in your area is uncomfortable, you ought to know about it. Follow through and follow up.
- Be informed. Take advantage of opportunities to learn about sexual harassment research and policies.
- Be willing to ask for help. If something comes up that you're not sure about, seek out someone who might know more.
- Be vigilant. Take every complaint seriously.
- Be a leader. Successful managers give leadership, not orders.
- Be proactive. Don't wait for a crisis. Look for opportunities to arrange trainings and discussions with your staff.

WHAT WOULD YOU DO?

The following scenarios represent the range of problems that managers can face. See which approach (or approaches) you would choose—and then take a look at the suggested responses.

Scenario 1

You notice that Hank is always rubbing Wendy's shoulders and making comments about the way she looks. You can tell Wendy is uncomfortable; she keeps her head down and her arms close to her sides during these encounters and never laughs or says thank you. You have announced on several occasions, both verbally and in writing, that staff members should feel free to come see you if they believe they're being sexually harassed, but Wendy does not seek you out. Do you wait for Wendy to say something to you? talk with Hank directly and tell him to stop? tell Wendy you can see she's uncomfortable and ask if she wants you to intervene? call both Wendy and Hank in to discuss the matter?

First, check in with Wendy. She may be keeping silent because she doesn't know how you'll regard the issue or because she doesn't want to get Hank in trouble. Reassure her that your conversation will be confidential. If she is uncomfortable with Hank's behavior, as you suspect, ask her what would be the best way for you to support her. She may feel after the discussion that she'd like to speak to Hank herself. You can discuss ways she could do this or recommend someone else she can talk to about it. Be sure to set a follow-up meeting and observe the situation carefully.

If Wendy wants you to talk to Hank, let her know that you will be raising your own concerns—not speaking for her. Then set up a meeting with Hank. Ask him if he thinks Wendy enjoys the attention and, if so, why he thinks so. Make him aware that many women would not want to be treated this way. Encourage him to examine the attitudes that lie behind his behavior. Does he view Wendy as a diversion from his work rather than a member of the team? Let Hank know you'll be glad to set aside time to discuss these issues with him further—but the bottom line is that he must change his behavior right away. If he seems resentful, make it clear that any hostile behavior toward Wendy will lead to discipline.

In a situation like this, you don't want to call Wendy and Hank in together. (If Wendy wants you present when she talks to Hank, she can call the meeting.) Sexual harassment is not a "personality conflict" in which both parties need to listen and be willing to compromise. Requiring a meeting of both parties makes it appear to be just that.

Scenario 2

Ray is your subordinate. At lunchtime, you stop by his office to leave him a note and find him sitting at his desk reading a pornographic magazine. Do you say nothing? rip the magazine out of Ray's hands? tell Ray you think it would be more appropriate to read it at home? call a department meeting to discuss pornography?

Ripping the magazine out of Ray's hands or calling a department meeting both make this out to be a more serious offense than it probably is. Ray is on his break and does have the expectation of privacy. Nothing in his behavior indicates that he intended to offend anyone. However, you should not ignore the incident. After all, if you walked in on Ray during lunch, someone else could as well. Ray needs to understand how uncomfortable many women feel when the man who is looking at them has just been looking at pornography. Anyone who does not wish to offend should be willing to do his reading off the premises. If Ray doesn't care how his female colleagues feel, let him know he will have to act as if he does.

Scenario 3

During your first year as manager, a company with which you do business sends all employees calendars with pictures of seminude women in provocative poses. The employees have been receiving these calendars for many years. Do you announce that this year the calendars will not be distributed? throw the calendars away? distribute the calendars? put a work group together to discuss the calendars and make a recommendation?

Distributing sexist calendars sends out the wrong message at a time when you're trying to increase sensitivity about sexual harassment. Putting the issue into the hands of a work group has some dangers. The group could decide that the majority of employees see nothing wrong with the calendars and want them distributed. On the other hand, making the decision without employee input can cause resentment.

A smart manager will encourage discussion but also provide leadership. Ask someone within the company or in your professional network who's knowledgeable on these issues to write a thoughtful memo; then have a work group meet to discuss it. If the department has not yet held a sexual harassment training session, this would be a good time to arrange one. You don't want people to think that such calendars represent the ultimate in sexual harassment. But you do want them to understand why the calendars are offensive to many people and why you oppose their distribution.

You can encourage members of the work group to write a letter to the company that sent the calendars. They can let company managers know they appreciate their business but are trying to improve the way women are viewed and treated in the workplace. In that spirit, they can urge the managers to design a new calendar, which they will be happy to distribute.

Scenario 4

John, who has been working in your area for five months, asks to see you. Because of his religious beliefs, he says, he finds profanity, the taking of the Lord's name in vain, and the expression "I swear" to be offensive. Do you tell John you'll send out a memo asking staff to refrain from using the language to which he objects? explain to John that the law does not protect the "hypersensitive" individual? ask John to be more flexible? call a department meeting to discuss the issue?

Technically, John is a "hypersensitive employee" whose wishes do not have to be met in order for you to comply with the law. However, most people, once aware of John's views, would be willing to watch their language—as they probably do with their young children or elderly relatives. The smart manager will ask John how he would like his feelings communicated to others in the department. Would he feel comfortable talking about the matter in a department meeting? You can also encourage John not to take it personally if the others forget once in a while. Bringing the matter up at a department meeting can help clear the air and encourage the rest of the staff to be mindful of John's concerns, without making them feel that every word out of their mouths is being monitored.

Scenario 5

Three men on your staff tell demeaning jokes about women, but only when the female staff members are not present. They are smooth about switching subjects if a woman enters the room. Do you tell them to cut the jokes out? send them to sensitivity training? say nothing? call a department meeting to discuss the issue?

Would these men tell racist jokes in front of a white manager if no person of color were in the room? (If the answer is yes, your company has another important issue to address.) They need to understand that some humor is simply degrading and not funny and, therefore, off limits, even if no women have overheard the demeaning jokes, so far.

Syndicated columnist Molly Ivins and other satirists make a clear distinction between ripping those in power (especially those who abuse their power) and making fun of those who are powerless. Making fun of Exxon after the Alaska oil spill or Vice-President Dan Quayle's remark while in Latin America that he should have studied Latin harder in school is very different from vulgar jokes about homosexuals and women. The former can be both funny and instructive; the latter are nothing but mean-spirited.

Scenario 6

Janice and Rick recently ended an affair. Now Rick has begun to date someone at another company. Everyone knows Janice is extremely jealous. She comes to you to file a sexual harassment complaint. Rick, she says, has been making lewd comments about her to the other guys. You suspect that Janice is lying. Do you listen carefully to Janice's complaint and follow the usual investigative procedure? tell Janice you think she's lying? pass the complaint on to your manager in order to ensure objectivity?

Your job as manager is to help resolve a conflict at the workplace. If the reason you suspect Janice is lying is that you have more knowledge than an outsider would, there is no reason to remove yourself from the process. There's a big difference between having an opinion based on information and being biased. Despite your suspicions, you should take Janice's complaint seriously. Pose questions that get at her feelings about the relationship. ("Did you have a prior relationship with Rick?" "Has that influenced you in any way?" "Why do you think Rick would make these remarks about you now?") If Janice is lying out of a desire for revenge, others who know the two people involved should be able to back up Rick's denials.

As a manager, you must always be alert to your own possible prejudices. Even if Janice is jealous and upset with Rick, she may *not* be lying. Rick may indeed be choosing an inappropriate way to express his anger at her. If an investigation isn't conclusive, make sure both parties know that lewd comments about a coworker will not be tolerated—and neither will false allegations. Proceed quickly and keep an eye on the situation.

Scenario 7

A group of male sales representatives comes to see you. They say they no longer want to be sent on out-of-town assignments with female colleagues because they are afraid of sexual harassment charges. Do you assure the men they don't have to travel with women? tell the men their fears are groundless? arrange for a sexual harassment training session? call a department meeting to discuss the matter?

Start by talking to the group of nervous men. Dispel the notion that women bring up sexual harassment complaints frivolously. Encourage the men to talk about what they themselves consider to be appropriate and inappropriate behavior on the road. Follow this session with a sexual harassment training session for the whole sales staff. They may want you to lay down some written guidelines, such as no visiting in one another's hotel rooms. A work group can help draw these up. The men need to understand that adopting a segregated travel policy might send the message that women are a hazard to the company and can't be treated as equals. The way to combat sexual harassment is not by avoiding contact but by practicing respect.

Scenario 8

The work group you manage engages in lighthearted sexual banter. Joan, a new employee, tells you she is not comfortable with the atmosphere. Do you talk to the others and ask them to tone it down? take Joan aside and talk to her about how she feels? call a meeting to discuss the situation?

It's best to prepare for possible changes in the work culture *before* a new person starts work. Make clear to the people in your department that banter has been allowed because it is light and okay with everyone but that you can't make assumptions about the new staff. You don't want her to feel that she has to go along in order to be liked or succeed on this job. In Joan's case, this groundwork apparently was not done. Call a meeting now and apologize for not having anticipated the problem ahead of time. Explain that both the law and common courtesy require respect for others' views. Let people know that you want them to enjoy the atmosphere at work and that there are other ways besides sexual banter to tease and joke. But the bottom line is, the group has to function as a team and get the work done as efficiently as possible.

As with John, who was offended by his coworkers' profane language, encourage Joan not to take it personally if people slip up, but make it plain that she has the right to work without offense. Everyone must be clear that neither offensive language nor any retaliatory behavior toward Joan will be tolerated. Check in frequently with Joan and with the others for a while. Practice what management consultant Tom Peters calls "management by walking around" to pick up on how things are going. If there is any backlash, deal with it quickly by calling in the individuals who are misbehaving and insisting they adhere to the new guidelines.

Scenario 9

After a sexual harassment training session, Arnie and Doug keep making jokes such as, "Sexual harassment—where do I get mine?" and "Hey, you brushed against my arm. I'm filing a sexual harassment charge." The women to whom they say this laugh and don't seem to mind. Do you take the women aside and ask them if they do mind? tell Arnie and Doug to stop? say nothing? call a department meeting to discuss the situation?

However harmless the intent may be, trivializing sexual harassment undermines an effective policy. Arnie and Doug need to understand what message their jokes send. Suppose someone were being harassed. In the context of such kidding, how likely would she be to come forward without fear of being ridiculed? Encourage the jokers to talk about the feelings behind their remarks. Help them see the difference between "lightening things up" and minimizing a serious problem. Remind everyone how harmful harassment can be. You can compare Arnie's and Doug's comments to joking about a blind person bumping into a wall at a time when the department is improving accessibility for the disabled. The formal structures won't be effective if employees undercut them by acting disrespectfully.

Scenario 10

Hazel has just lost a lot of weight. She starts coming to work in very short, tight skirts and clinging tops. Do you say nothing? call Hazel in to tell her to dress more appropriately? send Hazel a memo asking her to dress more appropriately?

You need to talk to Hazel, not send her a memo. Avoid any disparaging remarks about the clothes she's been wearing. Tell her that you understand why she might want to wear things she couldn't wear before she lost weight. But emphasize that she must adhere to the same dress code everyone else follows. You consider her a professional and want her to dress in appropriate business clothes.

Scenario 11

ABC Company is your biggest account. The buyer has been making unwelcome sexual advances to several women in your office. Do you ask the women to ignore it? tell the buyer not to come back? tell the buyer to change his behavior? call the buyer's boss?

Even though this buyer does not work directly for you, your company may be legally liable for his behavior. Furthermore, no account is worth demeaning your staff. But that doesn't mean you have to tell the offender never to cross your doorstep again. First, let the women in the office know you support them and are going to take action. Check with top management so that you can say you are speaking with their support. Then, talk to the buyer one on one. Make your views on his behavior clear. Explain that you could be sued for his behavior. Let him know that the account is important to you but not at the expense of your staff. Tell him that you'll go over his head if he doesn't change. This may be enough to get him to straighten out. If you do have to go to his boss, clarify what the law says—and also stress that a harassment-free environment is an internal priority for your company. If you have anything good to say about the buyer, pass that along as well, but make it clear that you expect him to shape up or be replaced as the representative to your office.

Scenario 12

The company issues a sexual harassment policy and says each manager should decide how to raise it with his or her staff. How would you proceed in a blue-collar workplace? in an office?

In either case, begin by sending a memo announcing that the company has adopted (or revised) a sexual harassment policy and that you're launching a campaign in the department to help implement it. Stress the commitment from top management and the goal: to make sure that the workplace is free from harassment and comfortable for both men and women. Let employees know that you're arranging for a sexual harassment training session where everyone will be free to raise questions and concerns. Encourage employees to answer an anonymous survey that you give out with the memo. The survey should ask whether employees have experienced harassment from supervisors, coworkers, clients, or customers; and whether they would feel comfortable reporting harassment. Share the survey results with whoever will conduct the sexual harassment training for your staff.

If your employees are unionized, be sure to work with the union in implementing the policy. If there is no union, ask for employee suggestions and for volunteers to help put the policy in place.

GUIDELINES FOR MANAGERS

Be a role model.
Be a good listener.
Be objective and consistent.
Be informed.
Be willing to ask for help.
Be vigilant.

10

What Every Good Employer Should Do

Sexual harassment will not be prohibited but it will be graded.

Poster at a stock brokerage firm

We tell people: it's harassment when something starts bothering somebody.

George Palmer, Du Pont Company

After the Clarence Thomas hearings in October 1991 and the passage of the federal Civil Rights Act shortly thereafter, many managers examined their policies on sexual harassment. What they saw ranged from an effective preventive program to no policy at all.

"A THRIVING WORKPLACE DEPENDS ON A HARASSMENT-FREE ENVIRONMENT"

Managers who promote this view are most successful in combating sexual harassment. Smart managers do want to avoid legal liability. But above all, they should root out anything that seriously interferes with employee morale, well-being, and productivity. They should recognize that sexual harassment can happen anywhere and that no matter how careful the hiring and promotion practices, no workplace has a guarantee against insensitivity or misconduct. They should work to prevent harassment from occurring, while dealing with it promptly if it does take place.

Managers in this category will understand that no employee is indispensable. Even if an employee brings in money or prestige, his misconduct should not be tolerated.

Many companies with well-developed policies, such as AT&T and Du Pont, have had them in place for more than a decade. Texas Industries began to develop its policy as soon as it started placing women in traditionally male jobs, such as driving and production engineering. While some companies began devising or reworking policies after the Supreme Court first ruled against harassment in 1986, firms like Merck & Co. said the ruling merely affirmed the policies they had already instituted.

NO POLICY AT ALL

Unfortunately, a significant number of workplaces—especially small and medium-sized firms—have no policy regarding sexual harassment. The absence of a policy reflects a variety of corporate views:

- "It's not a problem."
- "It's a problem, but not here."
- "I have too many other problems."
- "If you have a policy, you'll have a problem."
- "The problem isn't sexual harassment; it's government telling business what to do."
- "It's not *my* problem."

The "It's not *my* problem" view especially will drive away good employees. Consider the case of Sherry Ann. She was frequently subjected to foul language and dirty jokes at the insurance company where she did secretarial work. Nude pictures of men were placed on her desk. Sales agents rubbed her knee while she sat at the computer. One day, a sales agent yelled obscenities at her while backing her across the office—in the presence of her boss. When Sherry Ann confronted her boss about why he didn't intervene, he replied, "What'd you want me to do? Slug him?"

Sherry Ann left work and called the regional manager. "That's nothing new," he said dismissively. "I could tell you a lot more." Soon after, Sherry Ann quit her job.

One positive result of the Clarence Thomas hearings was new recognition of the seriousness of the issue. "I certainly had my awareness heightened to make sure that the environment is conducive to my employees' enjoyment and advancement," John W. Sauer, Conoco's chief energy analyst, told *Business Week* magazine (10/28/91). "The hearings will improve how companies follow up sexual harassment charges." Those with existing policies are strengthening them; others are eager to put a policy in place.

DEVELOPING OR REVISING AN IN-HOUSE POLICY ON SEXUAL HARASSMENT

There's no one model for a good sexual harassment policy. Employers need to develop procedures based on their particular circumstances. But all policies should be designed to send a clear message: "We will not tolerate sexual harassment. We will do everything in our power to prevent it from happening. If you have a complaint, we will listen to it. We will follow the most effective course of action to stop the offensive behavior as speedily and thoroughly as possible."

A good sexual harassment policy should incorporate the following elements:

Employee Involvement

Employees who have been or could be the targets of harassment should have a voice. Men who might otherwise feel defensive should also help to develop the policy. Rather than selecting one or two employee "representatives" at the outset, solicit comments and suggestions companywide. Through a union or professional association, some employees may know of a strong policy elsewhere; encourage them to pass on any information that may be helpful.

Once this material has come in, management will have an idea of who's interested in being part of a *work group*. The group should be multiracial, if possible, and include male and female representatives from all departments, both management and nonmanagement. It should continue to involve other employees as well.

The work group should design an anonymous survey to *find out what the existing situation is*. Avoid sweeping generalizations like "Have you ever experienced sexual harassment on this job?" Instead, ask a question like "Have you ever experienced any of the following behaviors?" and follow it with a list. Repeat the survey periodically.

Written Policy

A written policy tailored to the company should be included in any employee handbook and orientation materials. The policy should define what harassment is and is not, describe how harassment will be handled within the company, explain how to file a charge with a government agency, and spell out what the law says. But set *higher standards* than the law requires; for example, federal law does not prohibit harassment against homosexuals, but in-house policy should make clear that such harassment will not be tolerated.

Honeywell is an example of a company that replaced a vague policy statement with a detailed handbook on sexual harassment. The handbook spells out possibly inappropriate behaviors, including catcalls, sexual jokes, and staring.

Some management consultants advise employers to ban all sexual banter or romantic relationships among employees. Simply tell employees that such behavior is unacceptable and put an immediate stop to it, they say. But such an extreme policy may lead to resentment and misunderstanding on the part of employees. The purpose of sexual harassment policies is not to turn the workplace into a prison or managers into guards. The goal is to eliminate *unwelcome, offensive* behavior. An overly restrictive policy may lead employees to dismiss the effort and find ways to trivialize, or sabotage, company rules on harassment. For many people, the workplace presents an appropriate opportunity to meet eligible partners. It may seem less complicated just to forbid dating among coworkers, but in the end such a policy will backfire.

Publicity

Publicize the policy by every means used to communicate business goals. "Employers ought constantly to reinforce their commitment to a work force free from sexual harassment, using whatever the usual trusted mechanisms of the company are," says consultant Freada Klein. That could be anything from a newsletter to posters to global voice mail. "Some companies send a statement stapled to employee paychecks," says Klein. "Others send periodic memos about the number of complaints they've had and what the resolution has been."

Support from the Top

It's important to have visible support from top management. After the Thomas hearings, Richard Teerlink, the CEO of Harley-

Davidson, gave a ten-minute talk about harassment to the top 150 managers. "He talked very candidly and told us, 'This is serious stuff that goes along with our values of respecting the individual,'" said Margaret Crawford, director of the company's human resources department. " 'It's not just an issue of what's legal or illegal, but what's right and wrong and how do you treat people in the workplace. Managers will be held accountable for the environment your workers have to live in.' That ten-minute off-the-cuff presentation did more than anything else could have done. Word was out in the hallways. People came forward with questions, some situations they were uncomfortable about. They saw this as a very strong message that the company will not take harassment lightly."

Prevention

A successful policy depends on *education of all employees*. Training should be *ongoing*, not a one-time session, and presented *on paid time*. The program should aim to help all employees to understand the issues and the seriousness of the problem, ensure that those experiencing harassment know their rights, and inform any hardcore offenders that they won't get away with harassment.

"No Action Necessary" The insurance company where Tana worked adopted a sexual harassment policy on paper in 1989. Yet top managers continued to make sexually offensive remarks. Once, in the middle of a business discussion, Tana's boss changed the subject. "I love watching women eat bananas," he told her. On another occasion, he walked through the department remarking that "women wearing skimpy bathing suits deserve to be raped." Tana submitted a proposal advocating antiharassment education for all employees. Months later, the company's Action Committee reviewed her proposal and decided no action was necessary.

Training Programs Other companies, on the other hand, recognize the value of training programs for all levels of employees. Education sessions at Digital Equipment Corporation examine scenarios based on actual incidents that have occurred at the company. So does a training videotape created by a group of scientists at Corning, Inc.

Some argue that antiharassment education is a form of mind control, subjecting employees to whatever "politically correct" views are currently in fashion. Others worry that the more you encourage people to talk about sexual harassment, the more they'll start to see it all around them, whether it's there or not. Experience does not bear out these concerns. Good training encourages a free exchange of views—a key to combating harassment. Some employees may be afraid that anything they say may be construed as harassment; they need to hear that this is not true. The more information employees have, the better equipped they are to change their own behavior or to influence their coworkers.

Trainers should be carefully chosen; they can be either from within the company or from outside. The trainer should be able to deal with workers as well as managers. If harassment has been rampant, the trainer may need to meet with a few employees beforehand and enlist their help. One company brought in a consultant who treated all the men like dyed-in-the-wool harassers. Not surprisingly, most of the participants walked out of the session.

Clearly Defined Procedures that Protect the Complainant—and the Accused

The policy must clearly spell out the complaint procedures, including where to report problems, what steps will follow, timetables, methods of investigation, and follow-up. To maximize options for the complainant, the policy must allow for *several different channels*. The procedure should not require the complainant to report the problem to her supervisor, since that person may be the harasser. At least one option should be to complain to an employee through an affirmative action committee, women's committee, or other employee committee. If feasible, designate an ombudsperson to counsel victims. Du Pont Company has a sexual harassment hotline with a toll-free number listed in the company's telephone directory. Four staff specially trained in sexual harassment and rape prevention are assigned to the hotline; each carries a beeper.

The policy must state unequivocally that no one will be punished for coming forward and that *every* complaint will be taken seriously. No retaliatory action should be permitted against a complainant. But make clear, too, that false accusations will not be condoned and that *due process* will be followed.

In addition to formal channels, employees should have an *informal* way to check out their feelings or to ask someone else to observe whether harassment is taking place. Corning Inc., for instance, offers workers the option of a confidential outside consultant. An informal procedure should include a *timely follow-up meeting* to assess the situation and decide whether further action is in order.

Some companies, overly concerned about their legal liability, interpret the requirement for prompt and corrective action too literally; once they hear of a possible complaint, they feel they have to launch a full-scale investigation. That led to problems for Beverly, who wanted help dealing with the sexual advances of an outside contractor working in her office. She went to personnel to find out what the complaint procedure was. The personnel manager convinced Beverly to tell her the name of the harasser. The manager then announced that company policy required an immediate investigation. She insisted Beverly meet with the contractor right away in her office and make her accusations to his face. The next day Beverly was told she would be interviewed by the company's lawyer. She felt as if *she* were under investigation.

Mediation

In some cases, mediation is possible at the beginning of the process. If the harassment is not a long-standing problem, if the harasser seems open to discussion, and *if the complainant chooses this option*, a mediator can bring the parties together and try to resolve the conflict without a full-scale investigation.

Judy Bashor, Ombudsperson for Sexual Harassment at the Group Health Cooperative of Puget Sound in Seattle, Washington, sets strict groundrules when she uses mediation, following a highly structured process in which first one person speaks, then the other.

Bashor describes an incident in which a female nurse was subjected to verbal harassment from a male charge nurse and another male employee. The two men teased her about having a "hickey" and said they wouldn't mind giving her another. One of them followed her to the bathroom and kept up his remarks while standing outside the door. She was extremely upset. Others in the work group heard about the issue and began to take sides.

The female nurse opted for mediation after being counseled by Bashor. The male charge nurse was surprised to hear how upset she'd been. He was receptive to criticism and apologized. He felt he'd allowed the other male worker to affect his judgment. The two parties then discussed how to talk to other employees about the issue. They drew up a written agreement specifying that they'd say they had resolved the issue and didn't want to discuss it further. The agreement also stated that they would continue working compatibly and specified how they'd deal with any future issues.

Bashor also recommends "general warning" education. If an incident is reported that is vague or relatively mild, she might go to the work area and conduct a training session with the whole group. The purpose of the session is to stop the behavior and to encourage other people to come forward if necessary.

Prompt Investigation

Management should designate one or more specially trained employees who will carry out investigations. Du Pont assigns an investigative team of one man and one woman to each case; usually the investigators don't know the parties involved. "One of the most compelling messages . . . is how differently men and women perceive these issues," Du Pont manager Faith A. Wohl told *Business Week* magazine (10/28/91). Unions stress the importance of including employee representation so that employees will trust the process and not feel as if "the fox is guarding the chicken coop," as one union official put it.

Begin the investigation within seven days after a formal complaint is made. Help the complainant make her case, while guaranteeing due process for the accused. The process is *confidential*—remind all participants that they are not to gossip about the complaint. Keep a record of all meetings.

Interviewing the Complainant A written form can help complainants to organize their points and to be as concrete as possible about the who, what, where, when, and how of the allegations, as well as the ways in which they indicated the behavior was unwelcome and what impact the harassment had on their work.

Investigators should strive to set the complainant at ease and should explain exactly what the process will be like. While stressing that they need to remain objective, the investigators should reiterate the employer's strong position against sexual harassment. Their task is to enable the complainant to tell her story in as much detail as possible; they should seek to clarify facts, not to cross-examine or judge. They should avoid grilling the complainant. This is an investigation, not an interrogation.

Note that the investigator's questions in the following example are specific, and elicit specific answers from the complainant, without intimidating her.

Investigator:	Tell us who you feel has harassed you and in what way.
Mary:	Dwayne keeps commenting on my appearance and giving me suggestive looks.
Investigator:	What's his manner when he does that?
Mary:	He stands close to me, and his tone of voice is breathy and suggestive.
Investigator:	How does that make you feel?

The investigators should ask to see any evidence the complainant might have—memos, notes, graffiti, or the like. At the end of the interview, the investigators should summarize their understanding of the complaint and ask what remedy the complainant would like—an apology? discipline? a transfer for the accused? The complainant won't determine the kind of discipline used, but her opinion can be valuable.

Interviewing the Accused   No decision should be made before interviewing the accused. The investigators should have the job descriptions of both individuals and make sure they understand the work relationship between the two.

Investigators should tell the accused what has been alleged and listen carefully to his side of the story. He may deny that the behavior happened or that it was unwelcome. If the former, the accused person should be asked why he thinks he has been accused of the behavior and if he can suggest anyone who can corroborate his view. If the latter, the investigators should ask the accused to describe what made the behavior seem welcome.

The accused may say he didn't understand that his behavior would make anyone uncomfortable. Now that he does know, the investigators should find out what action, if any, *he* would suggest to correct the situation.

Interviewing Witnesses   Interviews should be conducted with anyone who might be able to support or contradict either side of the story. If the alleged harassment has occurred in private, as is usually the case, the investigators should talk with people who might have observed the complainant after an interaction with the accused. The investigators should try to ascertain if any other individuals experienced similar behavior from the accused, if the complainant confided in anyone while the harassment was going on, or if supervisors observed any behavior that might be relevant. Witnesses should be reassured that no retaliatory measures will be taken against them.

Recommendation   The investigators should consider whether the evidence suggests that harassment did take place and, if so, what discipline is appropriate. They should then make a recommendation to top management.

In "he says, she says" cases, the EEOC has ruled that the victim's word alone may prevail if it is sufficiently detailed and internally consistent to be believable. Still, sometimes it may not be possible to decide who's telling the truth. In that event, managers can reiterate the employer's strong stand against sexual harassment and against false accusations and let both parties know that management will be watching the situation. Whoever is lying will have been put on notice. If possible, managers can make sure that the individuals don't work alone together.

Experts agree that while false accusations are rare, they can occur. Generally, other employees will know if someone is out for revenge. A person who makes up an accusation should be disciplined, but management must be sure that the charge is false before taking such action.

Sheila worked in a large firm doing heavy, dirty work alongside men. For eight years, she experienced repeated sexual harassment. The company took little action. The only training was a 45-minute lecture on the "dos and don'ts" of sexual harassment.

When Sheila complained about a derogatory comment, her supervisor conducted what he called a "thorough investigation," which consisted of simply talking with the men involved, one of them a supervisor who had received a verbal warning for a previous incident involving Sheila. The men denied everything. The supervisor concluded that Sheila was lying and suspended her for one day for "false accusations." Sheila filed a grievance—and hired a lawyer.

Many managers would have taken a different approach and been less willing to believe the men, who might have had a stake in denying the charge. Even if it wasn't possible to prove Sheila's allegations, the manager should have put all parties on notice that neither sexual harassment nor false accusations would be tolerated. Then he should have arranged for sexual harassment training.

Discipline

Discipline can range from verbal and written warnings to formal reprimands, suspension, transfer, probation, demotion, or dismissal. Counseling may be appropriate.

The level of discipline should depend on both the nature of the harassment and the position of the harasser. Supervisors should be held to a higher standard, both because they represent the employer and because the control they exercise over a subordinate makes their offensive actions more powerful. A repeat offender should also receive a stiffer penalty.

Susan Geisenheimer, vice-president of human resources at Time, Inc., told *Working Woman* magazine about an incident in which a man at the company had been systematically harassing women on his staff for two years. When one woman complained, her female supervisor advised her not to "get into a room alone with him" and took no further action. After the complaint finally reached the human resources department, the man was fired—and the female supervisor received a warning for her inaction.

Punishment Should Fit the Offense Bill, a clerk, told Kathy, a secretary in his department, how sexy she looked in her sweater. After giving Kathy his address and phone number for a company insurance form, he said it was only fair that she give him her number as well and that he would be calling on Saturday night, even after Kathy made it clear she was not interested in him. Kathy told a manager about Bill's behavior. The manager called Bill in and asked him if Kathy's account of their conversation was correct. Bill said he didn't recall. Although there had been no other complaints about Bill's behavior (and no sexual harassment training had been done in the department), he was put on probation.

Managers trained in handling incidents of harassment would have given Bill a verbal or written warning and spent more time trying to get him to see what was wrong with his behavior. They also would have arranged for sensitivity training for the entire department.

Many employers take care not to reveal the reason for the discipline. But management should avoid any action that might imply that the harassment hasn't been taken seriously. Also, it's essential that management follow up with the *complainant* to make sure the behavior isn't repeated. If the resolution involves transferring the complainant, the move should be made only with her agreement and with clear guarantees that the new position will be equivalent or better in terms of pay, benefits, responsibilities, working conditions, and opportunities for advancement.

Follow-up should also be done with harassers—even if they are asked to resign—to make sure they understand what was wrong with their behavior. Management consultant Alma Baron told a group of Milwaukee business and professional women about a major corporation whose managers contacted her after being sued six times in the past three years. She described interviews she held with two men who had been terminated as a result of the suits. "The saddest part," said Baron, "was that these men still didn't know what they had done wrong. 'I've been doing this all my working life,' they told me."

Support for the Victim

The employer should make sure the complainant receives counseling during what may be a very difficult period in her life. People who have experienced sexual harassment sustain an injury. Even when the behavior stops, that injury may need healing. Victims should be referred to the employee assistance program, if any, as well as to outside resources (sexual harassment support group, rape crisis center, sexual assault treatment center, family counseling service, etc.). Victims of severe harassment might need to take some time off.

Monitoring

The employer must keep tabs on the process to make sure that the in-house investigators are fair and that there's no retaliation against complainants. Retaliation can include not only firing but also subtle isolation, poor reviews, and a change in work assignments.

Making managers responsible for preventing sexual harassment (as well as refraining from offensive behavior themselves) is essential to developing a successful policy. AT&T's policy states that "each supervisor will be held responsible for the prevention of such behavior on his shift and within his area of work responsibility." When managers pay lip service to eliminating harassment and then promote a harasser, they undercut the policy. Likewise, when managers reward the person who takes a stand against sexual harassment, they send a powerful message to all employees.

GOING THE EXTRA MILE

Managers with a deep concern for the damage caused by sexual harassment should accept a special challenge: Become *leaders*. Here are some steps to take:

1. Share your policy and the results of your anonymous survey with other business leaders.

2. Form a committee of like-minded managers in the local Chamber of Commerce to explore ways to encourage more attention to sexual harassment.

3. Develop a pledge for businesses to sign: "XYZ Company pledges to do everything within our power to eliminate discrimination from our work force. Our antidiscrimination policies and procedures are open for review." Such an effort would send a message to the community and to employees that combating sexual harassment and other forms of discrimination is a priority.

Do strong antiharassment policies work? Employers who have them believe they do. Preventive measures help reduce the number of complaints. Effective procedures resolve the charges that do get filed. Ken Carlson, director of equal employment opportunity for Amoco Corporation, says adding teeth to the in-house policy has practically eliminated any complaints being taken outside the company. "I can't recall one in the last 13 months this policy has been in effect," Carlson told the *Chicago Tribune* (10/29/91).

KEY POINTS OF A SEXUAL HARASSMENT POLICY

Involve employees.

Get support from top management.

Emphasize prevention through education and training.

Clearly define procedures to protect the complainant and the accused.

Give several options for reporting, including informal channels.

Investigate promptly, using a team of impartial investigators to interview accuser, accused, and witnesses.

Administer appropriate discipline, including counseling.

11

When Company Channels Don't Work: The Agency Process

A strong in-house policy can prevent or resolve most instances of sexual harassment. But some cases require the intervention of an outside agency. The agency complaint process is the government's way of saying to victims, "If the employer won't listen to you, we will. And we'll make sure management takes care of the problem."

WHEN AND WHY TO FILE A CHARGE

Under what circumstances should you file a formal complaint outside company channels? Generally, it's time to call on an outside agency if you've already tried bringing the problem to the attention of management and haven't gotten prompt or effective action. But in some cases, it's best not to wait until you've exhausted in-house channels. For one thing, there's a time limit on filing—a complaint with the federal agency, the Equal Employment Opportunity Commission (EEOC), must be made within 180 days of the incident of harassment. (You have up to 300 days in some states.) For another thing, filing your complaint with a government agency may help prod your employer to resolve the problem.

WHO CAN FILE

In order to fall under the jurisdiction of the EEOC (which handles sexual harassment charges under Title VII of the Civil Rights Act of

1964), the company you work for must employ 15 or more people. The employer can be a private company, state or local government, educational institution, or labor organization. Government bodies and educational institutions often have internal procedures that move more quickly than the EEOC. But even if you pursue internal channels, you can also file with the EEOC.

If you work for a firm with fewer than 15 employees, you must file with your state or local antidiscrimination agency if there is one. (Consult your telephone book under state and local government.) You don't have to have been fired or threatened with firing to file. If you have experienced sexual harassment, you are eligible to file, as long as you do so within the time allowed.

DO YOU NEED AN ATTORNEY?

You don't need an attorney to file a complaint with either a federal or state agency. But it's a good idea to consult one if you can afford the consultation fee or can find an attorney who offers free consultations. (See Chapter 7 for more on attorneys.) In particular, you want to know the following:

- How strong is your case?
- How have the local offices of the EEOC and state agency been handling complaints like yours?
- What should you include in your written charge?
- What can you ask for in the way of relief?

If you win or make a settlement with your employer, attorney fees can be included in the award. If you win damages, the attorney may be entitled to a percentage. The lawyer may also require some payment up front.

THE EMPLOYER: HOW TO RESPOND TO A CHARGE

A manager who receives notification that a charge has been filed against the company should find out whether any supervisor in that department was aware of a problem; begin an internal investigation, if none has already been done; and then take corrective action. Document all steps taken. Timely remedial action on the company's part can lead the complainant to withdraw the charge or cause the agency to close the case. An immediate management response will also deter future harassment—and future complaints.

THE EEOC PROCESS

The EEOC office closest to you is listed in the telephone book under *U.S. government*. (Also see Appendix B.) You don't need to make an appointment ahead of time.

Eligibility

The EEOC staff will begin by making sure your problem falls under the agency's jurisdiction. You will receive a sheet with precharge instructions. The sheet asks two questions: Is your problem illegal discrimination as a result of one or more of a list of reasons, including discrimination on the basis of sex? Do you believe an agency investigation will find proof that you were subjected to discrimination? If you answer yes to both questions, you will then be asked to fill out an intake questionnaire.

The intake form is quite detailed. It asks, among other things, for the reason the employer gave for the actions you are describing (e.g., if you were fired, what was the official reason given?) and for names of people who could serve as witnesses, along with a description of what they'll say. Check with your potential witnesses ahead of time to determine what information they can provide and if they are willing to be witnesses and to alert them to the fact that they may be contacted by an EEOC investigator. You can also supply witness names during the course of the investigation.

After filling out the questionnaire, you will meet with a staffperson who will decide if your case falls within the guidelines of the agency. For example, if the information on your questionnaire indicates that the incident happened two years ago, you'll be informed that it's too late to file.

If you are unable to go to the agency in person, you can write or telephone and ask that the forms be sent to you in the mail. Once you return the forms, agency staff will talk to you over the phone. Staff may also be able to arrange an appointment outside normal office hours. You may bring a friend along for support.

The Charge

Assuming that you meet the criteria regarding jurisdiction and time limits, you'll be able to file a charge. The charge form is far less detailed than the intake questionnaire. (See Appendix C.) It asks only for your name, address, and phone number; the employer's correct name and other identifying information; what kind of discrimination you experienced; and the date of the most recent incident. There is also space for you to write whatever particulars you want to include. Some EEOC offices provide assistance in filling out the charge; others don't have adequate staffing to do so. You are then referred to as the "charging party."

Your charge description should include:

- all the incidents of harassment
- how you indicated the behavior was unwelcome
- information on the harasser[s], including relationship to you on the job
- the effect harassment has had on your performance
- your efforts to inform management, if any
- instances of retaliation, if any.

Notification

The EEOC's guidelines require sending the charge, or complaint, to the employer within 10 days, along with a questionnaire about the allegations and a request for a response within 30 days. (The agency can grant extensions.) The purpose of the questionnaire is to gather evidence that will either refute or substantiate the charge. If the investigators receive no response, they'll follow up to find out why. If necessary, they'll issue a subpoena. It is illegal for the company to retaliate against a complainant. Any retaliatory behavior should be reported to the EEOC right away.

Fact-Finding Conference

In some cases, the agency may hold a fact-finding conference during which both parties tell their side of the story and try to reach an agreement. This conference is not the same as a hearing. There is no administrative law judge and no cross-examination. Only the investigator asks questions but may draw on suggestions from each party. First, the investigator reads the charge. Then the complainant describes what led up to the charge, and the company representative responds to the allegations. Each side may comment on what the other has said. EEOC investigators are not attorneys and are less strict than a judge would be about what kind of evidence may be considered. Verbal accounts of what other people said are admissible.

Investigation

If you don't reach an agreement at the fact-finding conference, the EEOC does a full investigation of the evidence on both sides. The investigation can include an on-site visit to the workplace to gather information.

The more evidence the charging party has, the stronger her case. It's helpful for the charging party to have kept a log of each incident. It also helps to find others who have been harassed by the same situation or individual. The employer's best defense will be to document steps taken to prevent harassment or to deal with the incident in question.

Witnesses may speak to an investigator anonymously, as long as the proceedings stay within the agency. If the case goes to court, however, their names will have to be disclosed.

Expedited Processing

In urgent cases, where the EEOC staff believe that irreparable harm could occur, a mechanism called *expedited processing* can speed up the process. In these rare cases, the agency immediately gets an attorney involved. The attorney works with the investigator to schedule interviews and to issue a questionnaire to management within a very short time frame in order to reach a determination quickly and get the case into court.

In one case in the Milwaukee district, a manager at an employment agency pressured a new hire to "pay him back" for helping her get the job. If she didn't sleep with him, the manager threatened, he would make her life difficult and ensure that she got no job referrals. The woman complained to the EEOC, which began an investigation and found a male coworker who had overheard some of the harassing conversations. The manager then threatened both the complainant and the witness with physical violence. The EEOC obtained a restraining order and concluded the investigation in only three weeks. An injunction—posted in the workplace and naming the manager—prohibited him and all other management personnel from threatening employees or subjecting them to sexual harassment or retaliation.

Determination

After the investigation is completed, the EEOC makes a determination of whether there is "reasonable cause" or "no reasonable cause" to believe that discrimination took place. If the finding is "no reasonable cause," the investigator will notify both the charging party and the employer. The charging party may request a review of the finding by the district director or deputy director. The staff will also give the charging party a "Right to Sue" letter, which allows her to bring a private lawsuit in court. A complaint must be filed in court within 90 days after a "Right to Sue" letter is issued.

The charging party may ask for a "Right to Sue" letter 180 days (or more) after the EEOC process begins, regardless of what stage the process is at and whether any determination has been made.

Conciliation

If the EEOC does find reasonable cause, the next step is to try to get the employer to agree to eliminate the discrimination and provide appropriate remedies. This stage is known as conciliation.

However, the agency can't force the two sides to conciliate. If the employer and the charging party can't agree on a remedy, EEOC lawyers may file a suit on behalf of the charging party. If the EEOC decides not to litigate, the charging party will receive a "Right to Sue" letter.

The EEOC appears to have a stricter standard than many state agencies and is often less likely than the state agency to find "reasonable cause." At one time, "reasonable cause" and "worthy of litigation" meant the same thing: If EEOC staff found reasonable cause for discrimination, that meant they were willing to have their own attorneys fight the case in court. Today, this standard is not the official position of the agency.

Going to Court

A complaint may wind up in court under one of the following conditions:

- The EEOC finds "reasonable cause." Conciliation fails. EEOC attorneys litigate the case in court.
- The EEOC finds "reasonable cause." Conciliation fails. The charging party gets a "Right to Sue" letter from the EEOC and, usually with the aid of an attorney, files the complaint in court.
- The charging party decides not to wait for the EEOC to make a determination. Once the agency has had the complaint for

180 days, the charging party asks for a "Right to Sue" letter and goes to court.

- The EEOC finds "no reasonable cause." The complainant decides, usually with an attorney, to ask for a "Right to Sue" letter and to pursue the case in court.

The court looks at the whole issue anew. The judge may or may not admit the EEOC finding into the record. *An EEOC finding of no reasonable cause, in other words, does not mean that the charging party will lose in court.* Many attorneys advise complainants to request a "Right to Sue" letter and proceed with a court action *before* the EEOC has made any determination. Unlike in a rape case, the victim doesn't have to prove beyond a reasonable doubt that the offensive behavior occurred. She just has to show by a "preponderance of the evidence" that the harassment *probably* happened. With the passage of the Civil Rights Act of 1991, which permits monetary damages for emotional suffering, more harassment victims may decide to pursue their cases in court. Some attorneys also use state tort laws to pursue sexual harassment claims. (See Chapter 3.)

PREPARING TO FILE—SOME HINTS

If you are considering filing a complaint with the EEOC or with a state agency, here are some suggestions that can help you and the agency:

1. Start by taking detailed notes on what has happened. Include every incident you can think of, with dates and descriptions of the nature of the harassment. Then pare the list down, picking out the most important examples. You want to be as concrete and concise as possible when talking to the intake staff, but don't leave out any relevant information.

2. Make a list of any possible witnesses. Also ask around for names of women who have left the company who might have had contact with the harasser.

3. Think about what you want for a remedy. If you were fired or forced to quit, you may feel that the last thing you want is to get your job back. Yet you might be entitled to reinstatement. If the harasser is disciplined or other circumstances change, you may decide that you do want to go back. Keep your

options open and ask for everything to which you are entitled. Under the 1991 Civil Rights Act, this can include any money you lost as a result of the harassment (e.g., back pay plus promotion), legal fees, out-of-pocket expenses, and possibly damages for pain and suffering. Be sure to get a legal opinion on whether or not you'll be able to ask for monetary damages other than back pay. And demand that the company adopt an effective sexual harassment policy, complete with mandatory training for all employees.

4. Understand that investigators can't take sides. Their job is to be neutral. Feel free to ask questions, but don't expect the investigator to act as your lawyer. The investigator also has no control over how large the backlog of cases is, but should be able to give you a reasonable idea of how long the process will take.

5. Take an active role in your case. Speak up. Ask questions. If you are not satisfied with your treatment, call the agency Compliance Officer or the District Director.

PITFALLS IN THE EEOC PROCESS

The EEOC process has helped many victims. But it has serious shortcomings.

• **Backlog.** Because of substantial funding cuts during the Reagan years, the agency is understaffed and has a heavy case backlog. Staffing dropped 24 percent in the 1980s. By 1990, the agency had a backlog of 41,987 discrimination cases nationwide. In some parts of New York, for example, complainants were told they might have to wait up to five years for their cases to be processed. Some complainants wait months before hearing anything at all from the EEOC—and then hear that their complaints have been dismissed.

• **Forms.** Intake and complaint forms can be confusing and intimidating. Furthermore, the wording of the precharge instructions is needlessly discouraging. The instructions read, "Do you think that if we investigate your charge we can find *proof* that you were subjected to discrimination for one or more of the reasons listed in Section 1?" Sexual harassment commonly happens without witnesses, and, by agency guidelines, a victim's word can constitute proof. The instructions, however, don't make this clear. Some offices offer assistance to complainants in filling out the forms; others don't.

• **Brochure.** The agency brochure doesn't provide a clear, easy-to-read description of what the agency process will be. What's needed is a document listing all steps in the procedure in simple language and the names and telephone numbers of key personnel, including the Intake Officer (who may also investigate the case,) the local Compliance Officer, and the District Director. The instructions should give an idea of the likely time frame for investigating a complaint.

• **Training.** The agency has no systematic approach to training or to overseeing cases. While most staff are well trained and sensitive, instances do crop up of staff who discourage filing of complaints, fail to return calls, or violate one or another of the agency's guidelines.

• **"Reasonable cause" standard.** Many attorneys feel the EEOC's "reasonable cause" standard needlessly dismisses many worthy complaints and should be reviewed. Fewer than 5 percent of charges filed with the agency in 1990 were found to have "reasonable cause"; in nearly 38 percent of the cases, "no reasonable cause" was found. (The rest of the cases were settled, withdrawn, or dismissed.) And only a small number of sexual harassment cases are taken to court each year by the EEOC. In 1990, for example, 5,557 sexual harassment cases were filed nationwide, but a total of only 50 were litigated.

STATE AGENCIES

Every state, with the exception of Alabama, Arkansas, Georgia, Louisiana, and Mississippi, has a state agency that addresses sexual harassment. Harassment victims who work in companies with fewer than 15 employees must use a state agency because the EEOC doesn't cover them. But even in a larger company, it may be advisable for a harassment victim to pursue a claim with the state agency, rather than the EEOC. State agencies often have a smaller backlog and move more quickly; and, while the EEOC is restricted from giving out documents it receives, most state agencies permit each party greater access to the information presented by the other.

State agencies can work very differently from the EEOC. In

Wisconsin, for example, as at the EEOC, an initial investigation results in a determination of either "probable cause" or "no probable cause" that discrimination took place. Then the state agency attempts to get the two sides to agree. But unlike the EEOC, Wisconsin has a hearing process. If conciliation fails, the case goes to a hearing presided over by an administrative law judge. This hearing, like a trial, relies on formal rules of evidence. Both parties and any witnesses are examined and cross-examined by the attorneys for each side. (If either side has no attorney, the examination is carried out by the administrative law judge.) The judge then writes a decision, generally within 90 days. The decision contains findings of fact, points of law, and either an order of remedy or an order dismissing the complaint. If discrimination is found, the remedy can include back pay, reinstatement, attorney fees (if appropriate), and an order that the harasser "cease and desist."

Some states allow for damages for pain and suffering. If no damages are allowed, the charging party can write to the EEOC for a "Right to Sue" letter and go to court to seek further damages.

FEDERAL EMPLOYEES

Federal employees use separate procedures to file discrimination complaints. The time frame is shorter—a charge has to be filed within 90 days of the most recent occurrence. Forms are available through the EEO office in every federal agency.

ROLE OF ADVOCATES

Advocacy groups such as women's organizations and rape crisis centers can play a useful role.

- Advocates can make referrals to therapists, family counseling services, and attorneys. They may know of lawyers who will do a free consultation, take cases for no fee or on contingency, or have relevant experience.

- If the victim can't afford an attorney, advocates can discuss her case with her and inform her about what's involved in filing a complaint.

- In some cities, sexual harassment support groups can provide a "buddy" to support the victim while she goes through the complaint process.

- Advocates can help harassment victims speak up to EEOC personnel if they believe their cases are not being handled properly.
- If advocates hear of problems with the local EEOC or state agency, they can bring the situation to the attention of higher-ups or even the media.

The agency complaint process was designed as a safety valve to protect the rights of victims and enforce the law. With more resources and greater accountability, the antidiscrimination agencies can better fulfill this role.

THE AGENCY PROCESS

A person who works for a firm of 15 or more is eligible to file with the EEOC.

Anyone may file with a state agency; all but five states have antidiscrimination laws.

You don't need a lawyer to file a complaint.

The complainant may ask for a "Right to Sue" letter 180 days (or more) after the EEOC process begins, regardless of what stage the process is at, and pursue the case in court.

EEOC staff can speed up the process if they believe irreparable harm may occur.

12

What Every Good Union Should Do

It's not funny.
It's not flattery.
It's not your fault.
It's sexual harassment.
It's against the law.

> *Poster distributed by the Coalition of Labor Union*
> *Women (CLUW)*

Unions are an important part of efforts to combat sexual harassment. The issue fits squarely what unions are all about: to promote dignity, equality, and respect for all workers. And the collective bargaining structure gives workers the means to engage in serious discussions with management and to win real protections.

Yet, like virtually every other institution in our society, unions have been led by men, who, as a group, have not suffered sexual harassment first hand. Labor's track record on fighting sexual harassment is uneven. Some unions have been at the forefront of efforts to eliminate harassment; others have barely recognized the problem.

In championing the fight against sexual harassment, the union's main goal should be to protect its members against discriminatory treatment. To accomplish that, the union needs to work with management toward an effective policy and to use the union structure to mobilize the members to combat harassment. Committed unions have developed a systematic approach to fighting sexual harassment, pressing management to take action, educating union members, and training union leaders to deal effectively with the problem.

WORKING WITH MANAGEMENT

Antidiscrimination Clause

The first task is to get a strong antidiscrimination clause in the contract. Many contracts already have such a provision. Because sexual harassment is a form of sex discrimination, the clause ensures that sexual harassment will be covered by the grievance procedure. Instead of going through a lengthy EEOC process, someone who experiences harassment can simply file a grievance and ask for immediate relief.

Because a sexual harassment complaint may require greater confidentiality than other issues, some modifications of the grievance procedure may be needed. The union can suggest that any arbitrator used for sexual harassment cases will have received special training or have previous experience. And the union can seek to include sexual harassment grievances among those eligible for an "expedited procedure," skipping the initial steps of the grievance process.

Sexual Harassment Policy

The union can work with management to develop a sexual harassment policy that includes a definition of sexual harassment and a strong commitment by management to assure a harassment-free environment. While the antidiscrimination clause serves as a prohibition against sexual harassment, a company can also take positive action to prevent harassment from occurring in the first place. The policy can establish the option of an informal procedure, designating one or more persons to whom workers can go in confidence to try to resolve a sexual harassment problem without filing a formal grievance. Some unions recommend developing the sexual harassment policy during ongoing labor-management meetings, if any, rather than during contract negotiations, which may be perceived as a more adversarial setting.

Survey

As part of the sexual harassment policy, union and management representatives can design an anonymous employee survey to gain a better understanding of the nature and extent of the problem.

Training

The union should be part of joint efforts with management to arrange training sessions on sexual harassment. Union representatives can help identify training needs, help research and choose outside consultants if necessary, and help develop educational materials. Training sessions for union members should be held separately from management and on paid time.

New and Exempt Workers

The union can negotiate for the right to file antidiscrimination grievances for probationary or exempt (nonunion) workers. Such workers may be vulnerable to sexual harassment because they are less aware of their rights and more susceptible to pressure from a supervisor who has the power to terminate them. A hostile environment for workers who are outside the bargaining unit can have an impact on union members as well and falls within the scope of union concerns.

SUPPORTING PUBLIC POLICY EFFORTS

The union can support legislative efforts to expand protection for victims of sexual harassment. Laws requiring companies to provide education and training, for example, or laws broadening penalties for employers who allow harassment will help the union's efforts at the workplace. Unions should also lobby to make it easier for victims of sexual harassment to collect unemployment compensation if they leave a job.

WORKING WITH UNION MEMBERS

Many unions, at the urging of women members, are developing internal programs against harassment. Some wait until there's a crisis; others begin well before they have a problem. A model union program educates members to treat each other fairly, to use the grievance structure effectively, and to press management to create a harassment-free workplace.

The message to the membership is twofold: first, union principles demand a strong stand against sexual harassment because discrimination divides workers, building disunity and distrust; and second, combating harassment is a matter of saving jobs. The victims' jobs are only half the story. Harassers are sometimes union members, and management is required by law to take prompt corrective action against harassment—including firing the offenders. "I tell union leaders, you don't have to like this policy," says Dottie Jones, a United Auto Workers (UAW) staff member who coordinates sexual harassment training. "But if you care about your members, men *and* women, get involved. Otherwise you can't protect their jobs."

Any effort to deal with sexual harassment systematically must be *well organized* and *well led*. It must have strong support from the top, as well as involvement of stewards and rank-and-file members.

The Basics

Make sure that all union members know what to do if they're harassed. Tell them to let the harasser know clearly that the behavior must stop, to talk to the union representative, to seek emotional support, to document every incident of harassment, and, if the offensive behavior continues, to make use of the procedures that exist. (See Chapter 7 for more detail.)

A Special Committee

Ruth Needleman, education director of the Service Employees International Union (SEIU), recommends that efforts to combat sexual harassment *not* be led by the Women's Committee. "Sometimes the Women's Committee lacks authority within the local," says Needleman. She recommends forming a committee that includes top officers and respected stewards, as well as members who are especially interested in the issue. The committee should include both men and women and should also reflect the racial makeup of the membership.

The committee should begin by holding a far-reaching strategy session to examine how sexual harassment has affected the local and to set goals and objectives.

Leadership Training for Women

A structure needs to be established, if it does not yet exist, where women can be trained in assertiveness and leadership skills.

Women must be encouraged to share stories and gain courage by learning they're not alone and not at fault. A strong showing of interest from women members will help get top leadership to take action.

Training for Union Officials

The UAW's Dottie Jones warns of the hazards of confining harassment training to women members. "Most of us have been operating backwards," says Jones. "We've gone in and done numerous workshops at women's conferences for women's committees. We do need to reach them. But training at the top level is the true trickle-down." At the International level, training should be done for International reps, regional directors, and field staff. At the local level, the Executive Board must have a firm grasp of the importance of the campaign.

Training for the Grievance Committee and Shop Stewards

Ruth Needleman of the SEIU describes the process as "deputizing" the stewards, delegating them to have more authority in the fight against sexual harassment. They need to be turned into activists, not just apprised of the dos and don'ts.

In her training sessions for union leaders, Dottie Jones personalizes the issue for male union members by linking it to the American dream of having your kids go to college and do better than you. Jones describes the following scenario to the men:

> Your daughter is at college. She calls home and says, "Daddy, guess what happened today. A bunch of guys made a circle around me. They unzipped their pants, took out their penises, and wouldn't let me out of the circle until I exposed my breast. So I did. It was the only way to get out of the circle. Now I'm so humiliated and embarrassed, I want to drop out of school."

Imagining this scene, the men are understandably outraged. Jones lets them talk for a while. Then she points out that the same kind of thing is happening in the workplace. They're condoning it by not doing anything about it, she says; and in some cases, they're participating in it. "Every woman in the shop is also someone's daughter," Jones reminds them.

Jones also challenges the prevalent view that harassers are just acting on biological urges or that victims are asking for it. She gives participants these guidelines to judge their behavior and that of other men: "Would you behave the same way if your daughter or wife were here? if you were on TV? Would you put this poster in your living room? your daughter's bedroom?" She compares "girlie" posters to pictures of the Ku Klux Klan's Grand Dragon or Adolf Hitler, which the men generally accept as being out of line in the workplace. "There's not a separate dues pot and separate rights for women and men," she tells them. "The union is here to protect all workers."

Every union member needs to attend training sessions like this and receive regular refreshers. "We've been much more intentional about these activities in recent years," says Joyce Kornbluh, a labor educator who cochaired Michigan's Task Force on Sexual Harassment in the mid-1970s, the first of its kind in the nation. "But men still need to have their consciousness raised as to what's acceptable and what isn't. We can't take for granted that we've had a campaign against sexual harassment, so it's all wrapped up and everyone understands the problem."

Visible Commitment

A strongly worded union resolution informs every member about the union position on sexual harassment, and official bumper stickers, buttons, posters, and other paraphernalia help make the union's commitment visible. Many unions have printed materials on what the union and its members can do to fight sexual harassment on the job. The UAW created a logo featuring the face of the Statue of Liberty with the message, "When I *say* NO, I *mean* NO. Sexual harassment is against the law." In addition to buttons and bumper stickers, the union made a poster describing why victims don't talk about sexual harassment, how to stop it, and what the UAW is doing. The union's *Solidarity* magazine, sent to more than one million members, printed the poster as its back cover.

Beyond Rhetoric into Action

In Canada, the United Steelworkers Union begins *every* conference and convention, whatever its topic, with a presentation defining what sexual harassment is and stating that it will not be tolerated at that meeting. Anyone violating this rule, it is announced, will be sent home, and a letter will be sent to the local Executive Board detailing why.

A Clear Role for Men

The Australian Federated Clerks Union distributes a brochure entitled "Sexual Harassment Is Men's Business." The pamphlet makes several suggestions:

- "Don't stay silent when you see another man harassing a female workmate.
- "Don't laugh at jokes which degrade women.
- "Don't whistle at women in the street or let your mates think it's ok.
- "Be aware of your own behavior and whether it might be making women feel pressured."

An Organizing Issue

The SEIU made sexual harassment a central issue in its successful fight to organize workers employed by a maintenance contractor at Apple Computer. While sexual harassment may occur in unionized companies, said Jon Burton, coordinator of SEIU's campaign, "in nonunion companies, it's the Wild West—anything can be done. When there's a union, rules and regulations are much more carefully watched by management; there's training for supervisors; and we have union stewards in the buildings." In June 1991, SEIU organized a public hearing on conditions at the nonunion subcontractor; at the hearing, several women workers spoke out about vulgar sexual comments and requests for sexual favors.

WHAT IF THE HARASSER IS A UNION MEMBER?

If a manager harasses a member, the procedure is clear. The union helps the member file a grievance, if she chooses to, and supports her in finding an appropriate remedy. But what if one union member harasses another? Union activists encourage victims of coworker harassment to go to the union first.

Most union constitutions have provisions for dealing with internal conflicts between members. The union may designate certain people to handle harassment complaints and provide confidential counseling and support. In Canada, the Steelworker locals designate a Sexual Harassment Complaints Coordinator.

If a union investigation finds that harassment has indeed occurred, the leadership can immediately advise the harasser to stop the behavior and apologize. They may recommend counseling or training. Often the matter can be resolved without further action.

But if the harasser refuses to go along with the union's recommendation or if he agrees but then repeats the behavior, the victim can then bring the problem to the attention of management for disciplinary action. While the union has a duty to represent all its members—including the complainant and the accused—it has no obligation to file a grievance without merit. The union can file a grievance for the harasser if the discipline seems too harsh but cannot protect the member from being disciplined fairly for offensive behavior. As the Canadian Steelworkers put it in their sexual harassment policy, if internal union mechanisms fail, "persistent sexual harassment of a worker by a fellow worker must be regarded by the union as a circumstance which justifies the imposition of some discipline."

A Wayward Worker

A man walked up to a new female employee and announced, "I'm going to suck on your tit." The company gave him a three-day layoff. He went to his union steward and said he wanted to file a grievance. "Did you do that?" the steward asked. The man replied that he had. "Is there anything else I should know?" asked the steward. The man said there was not. The steward explained that the contract clearly prohibited harassment and that the worker had been warned of such behavior before. No grievance was filed.

A member found guilty of violating the rights of another member can also be brought up on internal charges under the union bylaws and constitution. The person can then be prohibited from running for union office or, if he is an officer, removed from that position.

In some cases, a union investigation may not be conclusive. In that event, the union does have the duty to represent both members. Different stewards can be assigned to each person so that both parties feel there's no conflict of interest. While making sure that the investigation is thorough and fair, the union should reiterate its strong opposition to sexual harassment.

HOW CAN I GET MY UNION TO COMBAT SEXUAL HARASSMENT?

If your union has not addressed the issue of sexual harassment, start by talking to other women. The UAW's Dottie Jones calls it "walls, halls, and stalls." How have women won any change? she asks. By talking to each other behind walls, in the halls, and in bathroom stalls.

You don't have to wait until you're harassed to press the union to take action. If you're a rank-and-file woman, talk first to the women to whom you're closest. It shouldn't be hard to find someone who agrees with you. Two or more of you can then approach the steward who's likely to be most sympathetic and find out how he or she feels. In other words, organize!

Once you have a steward on board, go to the highest-ranking union leader you can find who's likely to support you. Keep approaching people one on one, involving everyone you can. By the time you make a recommendation to the Executive Board, you should have one or more members of the Board involved, some ideas about how to achieve your goals, and a showing of interest within the local.

Do your homework on resources that might be available from your International. Building a campaign is a lot easier if the International has a supportive woman in a high position. But there are enough examples of sexual harassment programs throughout the union movement to help you, even if they're outside your own International. The Coalition of Labor Union Women acts as a resource and referral network, distributing useful materials on this issue. (See Appendix A).

Be prepared for resistance. Some people will accuse you of blowing the problem out of proportion. Others will agree that sexual harassment is bad but will wonder why women can't just take care of it on their own. Persevere!

If you have a specific harassment complaint and your steward doesn't take it seriously, says Dottie Jones, go over his head, higher in the union structure, until you find someone who *will* pay attention. And make sure you know your rights. "If you don't know your rights by union contract, union constitution, and law," Jones emphasizes, "your rights tend to be violated."

A successful union effort against harassment has valuable side effects. Women who share stories with one another and develop their leadership skills often go on to play important roles on other union issues. In this way, a well-organized campaign strengthens not only the women but the union as well. Members who learn to communicate with each other about harassment will be a stronger unit. And combating discriminatory treatment against women protects all workers against arbitrary or unfair treatment.

HOW UNIONS CAN COMBAT HARASSMENT

In combating sexual harassment, the union's main goal is to protect its members against discriminatory treatment. Unions can work with management to do the following:

- Include a strong antidiscrimination clause in the contract.
- Develop a policy that defines sexual harassment and spells out a strong commitment by management to assure a harassment-free environment.
- Arrange training sessions on sexual harassment.
- Negotiate for the right to file antidiscrimination grievances for probationary or exempt (nonunion) workers.

The union should mobilize its members and support legislative efforts to expand protection for victims of sexual harassment.

13

How to Get Your Employer to Adopt a Sexual Harassment Policy

Two clerical workers at a small Las Vegas collection agency were offended by sexually explicit jokes made by the firm's president. They consulted their personnel manager, who encouraged them to meet with the boss and write him a letter spelling out their complaint. He thanked them for bringing the matter to his attention and made it clear to all employees that dirty jokes, including his own, would no longer be tolerated in the office.

A strong workplace policy is the best way to combat sexual harassment. What if your company doesn't have one? Depending on where you work, you may very well be able to encourage your employer to adopt a new policy or make improvements in the one already in effect. It's worth trying—the policy changes you propose will benefit men and women employees and management alike. And the very process of pressing for a policy change can promote understanding of harassment throughout the company.

Being involved in winning a new policy can be therapeutic for anyone who has personally experienced harassment. Of course, in some cases, your best option may be to remove yourself from a dangerous and traumatic situation by leaving the company. But in other cases, staying on and winning a strong harassment policy can help you put your experience to constructive use and rebuild your sense of personal power.

SEEKING SUPPORT

Unless you work in a one-employee office, you probably won't want to go in to see the boss all by yourself. Most efforts toward an effective company policy begin with informal discussions among friends—on break time, in the company cafeteria, before or after work. Some people are interested in establishing an effective company policy because of their past or present experiences with harassment. Others, men included, are interested simply because they believe a clear policy will be best for everyone.

Once you and your friends have traded views and stories informally, you may want to reach out to people in other departments. Look for one or more sympathetic managers—male or female—who can advise you about whom to see, what approaches will be most persuasive, and which other managers will support you.

DIFFERENT KINDS OF WORKPLACES

Give some thought to *why* your particular workplace has an inadequate sexual harassment policy—or no policy at all. Managers at your company may simply have neglected to institute a policy. Or they may believe for one reason or another that the current policy, or the lack of one, is best for the company.

Some managers, like the Las Vegas collection agency president described at the beginning of this chapter, are more than willing to take action once the idea is brought to their attention. Others are more difficult to persuade. Sometimes involving the board of directors can be helpful; or, if the company is a branch of a larger firm, higher-ups from the parent company can intercede. And sometimes the only way to get a policy adopted is to go outside the company.

MAKING YOUR CASE

If management at your company needs persuading, stress these points:

• **Every workplace needs a policy.** Sexual harassment occurs throughout the work world. If it hasn't occurred at your company already, it might in the future. Harassment can escalate and become a serious problem. (If harassment is already a problem at your company, say so. Give examples.) Women who have been or are being harassed need to know how to find relief and redress. Men who are unsure about what constitutes harassment need guidelines.

• **It's the law.** EEOC guidelines specify that employers *must* take positive steps to prevent harassment and have a grievance procedure in place. An effective policy will reduce a company's legal liability. It will help solve problems before they become legal charges. And if a case does go to court, the employer will be on far stronger legal ground if a sound harassment policy is already in place.

• **Not having a policy is dangerous.** An employer is held liable for the actions of all managers and supervisors. With the passage of the Civil Rights Act of 1991, federal courts, as well as some state courts, can assess damages against the employer.

• **It saves money.** Sexual harassment tends to take a toll on the victim's work performance. Even the *fear* of harassment can reduce productivity. Dealing with harassment promptly and effectively or, even better, preventing it cuts down on absenteeism and turnover, improves morale, and avoids expensive lawsuits. Training by a sexual harassment consultant quickly pays for itself.

• **Other employers are doing it.** Leading companies have sexual harassment policies. Adopting a policy doesn't mean advertising that your company has a problem with sexual harassment. Rather, it shows that you are committed to creating a work environment that's hospitable to men and women alike.

• **It promotes effective working relationships.** A good sexual harassment policy reduces suspicion and fear among men, women, and their bosses.

PUT IT IN WRITING

If your company has no harassment policy at all or if your informal efforts are rebuffed, it can be helpful to spell out your proposal in a memo. You can outline your proposal in a letter that requests a meeting with management, or you can first schedule the meeting and then prepare a written proposal to present in person when you get there. Gathering signatures on your proposal, from men as well as women, can help promote discussion of the issue. In some situations, you might want to distribute copies of your statement or post it on the bulletin board.

In 1991, the National Women's Political Caucus sent a model policy to all 535 members of Congress and asked them to agree to outlaw harassment in their offices. Two hundred members agreed right away, and more did so after the Clarence Thomas hearings in October 1991.

WHOM TO APPROACH?

Once you've put your proposal down on paper, approach the person or persons with the power to put it into action. In some workplaces, the choice is obvious either because there's only one boss or because job titles are spelled out precisely. If you're not sure whom to meet with, ask around among coworkers or start with a sympathetic manager who can lead you to the right person.

- You might approach your immediate boss first, ask for his support, and inform him if you plan to speak with his superior.
- The personnel director, if any, may be the right person to go to.
- If your company has an affirmative action or equal opportunity office, try it as well.
- Going straight to the top can also be effective.

Don't spend too much time agonizing over which manager to approach. You might even approach several simultaneously.

MEETING WITH MANAGEMENT

Depending on the size of your company, *meeting with management* can mean two employees sitting down with the owner of the firm or a gathering in the personnel director's office of two dozen representatives from various departments and branches. No matter how formal or informal your meeting, be sure to prepare for it ahead of time.

- Plan to describe the problem, propose your solution, and end with specific requests.
- Decide who will speak and in what order.
- Appoint someone to take notes.
- Try to anticipate what the manager with whom you meet will say and practice how to respond.

- Plan to keep the meeting brief and businesslike. (Sometimes it helps to send the manager a brief agenda ahead of time.)
- If the manager wishes to take your proposal under consideration, ask him to get back to you by a certain date, say, a week or two later.
- Offer to help carry out whatever next steps are necessary.

HOW WILL MANAGEMENT RESPOND?

Many managers will receive your proposal enthusiastically and take prompt action. Some, on the other hand, may not welcome proposals from employees or may feel threatened by the topic of sexual harassment. They may need time to talk with other managers or employees before responding.

The federal Civil Rights Act of 1964 prohibits employers from retaliating against employees for taking action against discrimination (including sexual harassment). Employees who act as a group are also protected by the National Labor Relations Act. If you think you might need this legal protection, it's a good idea to keep a record of your actions against harassment, as well as written evidence of your satisfactory job performance.

No matter how your manager reacts initially, there's a good chance he'll end up accepting your proposal in some form—if you persist.

STAY INVOLVED

After your meeting, plan to help put the new policy in place and to keep tabs on how it's working. If your company sets up a committee or work group on harassment, make sure employees are represented. Once the program begins, members of your group can help answer these questions:

- Is harassment still occurring?
- Is management responding appropriately?
- Do victims need more support?
- Is the policy clearly understood by everyone at the workplace? Is it publicized and circulated periodically?

Be sure to celebrate any progress you make. And keep your group intact. What you learn from this experience may apply to other workplace issues as well.

IF YOU GET NOWHERE

If your employer is unresponsive, consider going outside the company. Approach an advocacy group, seek advice from a union, call the media, or take harassment cases to the EEOC or other legal body.

For Linda Schultz, filing a charge with the state fair-employment agency was the means to winning a policy at her company. As an electronic equipment saleswoman in California's Silicon Valley, Schultz developed frequent headaches, nausea, and higher blood pressure in reaction to her boss's relentless use of profanity, crude jokes, and sexual remarks about women employees. Her doctor advised her to quit her job. Instead, she filed a complaint with the California Department of Fair Employment and Housing. As a result, her boss and other corporate officers were ordered to attend training sessions on sexual harassment and to implement a policy against harassment.

"I'm told that women all over the state posted stories about my case on company bulletin boards," Schultz says. "That makes me feel good."

A STRONG WORKPLACE POLICY

A strong workplace policy is the best way to combat sexual harassment. If you work in a company with an inadequate policy or none at all, take these steps:

- Seek support from other employees and from sympathetic managers.
- If management needs persuading, stress that a harassment policy 1) will benefit all employees, 2) is required by law, 3) prevents legal and financial problems, and 4) promotes good work relationships.
- Offer to help implement the new policy. Monitor the policy to make sure it's effective.
- If management doesn't respond to your efforts, consider approaching an advocacy group, union, or government agency.

Remember: Management probably *will* accept your proposal in some form, if you persist!

14

Combating Sexual Harassment: What You Can Do

Offensive behavior *can* be eliminated from the work world—but only if everyone takes action. Here are some steps to take today to combat sexual harassment:

WHAT YOU AS AN INDIVIDUAL CAN DO

- Recognize the seriousness of the problem.
- Become informed and help inform others.
- Get support and speak up if you're being harassed.
- Offer emotional support to harassment victims; applaud them for speaking up.
- Don't engage in or condone behavior that demeans women.
- Let harassers know their behavior is offensive to *you*, as well as to the victim.
- Press for a strong harassment policy at your workplace and for other policies that promote fair working conditions.
- Keep sexual harassment in the public eye—write a letter to your newspaper; join an advocacy group active on the issue.
- Urge your local school district to instruct students in job rights and proper workplace behavior.

- Be a good citizen: Write letters to your government representatives and testify in support of strong legal protection for harassment victims. Let candidates and public officials know your views on the issue.

WHAT YOU AS AN EMPLOYER CAN DO

- *Adopt a strong harassment policy.* It should include an effective in-house complaint procedure, fair treatment of accuser and accused, and appropriate discipline. With an annual written notice, inform all employees of their rights, of complaint procedures, and of ways to file complaints with a state or federal agency.

- *Emphasize prevention.* Provide on-site training sessions or other forms of education about harassment for all employees. Make clear that harassment will not be tolerated.

- *Hold harassers accountable for their behavior.* Without seeking to avoid your own liability for harassment, you should explore ways of making harassers financially responsibile for their actions. (Courts can help. In 1979, in *Kyriazi v. Western Electric Co.*, the New Jersey District Court ordered a group of harassers and their supervisors to pay the victim $1,500 apiece, out of their own pockets.) See to it that serious harassers also suffer serious career consequences, whether through firing, demotion, or other penalties.

- *Elevate women's status in the workplace.* Sexual harassment grows out of women's inferior status in the work world. You should help women move into jobs held traditionally by men by eliminating discrimination in training and hiring, help men move into women's jobs by upgrading pay for jobs dominated by women, help women move into top management, and adopt "family-friendly" policies, such as family leave and child-care assistance.

WHAT UNIONS CAN DO

At every workplace, a union can work with management to include an antidiscrimination clause in the union contract and adopt a strong policy against harassment. Your union can educate and mobilize members to combat harassment and support legislative efforts to expand protection for victims.

HOW THE LEGAL SYSTEM CAN BE IMPROVED

Every level of the system that enforces laws against harassment can be improved. These changes will help:

- *Require employers to emphasize prevention.* EEOC guidelines state that employers must take positive steps to discourage sexual harassment, but the agency doesn't enforce this directive. Employers should be *required by law* to develop a clear policy against harassment. The State of Maine has already passed a law requiring employers to provide employees with education about harassment and a written notification of the harassment policy.

  Because many companies have already adopted harassment policies on their own, some business groups will argue that mandating them is unnecessary. In the words of conservative activist Phyllis Schlafly, "People don't need a federal policeman standing at every water cooler." In fact, however, employers who have already adopted harassment policies should welcome a requirement that other employers do the same. And those who haven't yet gotten on board can use a push in the right direction.

- *Speed up agency proceedings.* As more companies begin to deal effectively with harassment on their own, the need for legal action will decrease. But in the meantime, as awareness of harassment goes up, so will the number of cases filed. In the three weeks following the Clarence Thomas hearings in October 1991, the number of harassment cases filed at the EEOC increased by 23 percent.

  The agencies are already overwhelmed. The EEOC has a large backlog, and many state agencies are so overburdened that they routinely fail to meet the deadlines spelled out in their own regulations.

  Both the EEOC and the state agencies should aim to investigate every complaint within three months of filing. At least temporarily, they need extra funding for additional staff, including litigators.

- *Extend the statute of limitations.* Some harassment victims who file charges under federal law must do so within 90 days of the incident; others have up to 300 days to file charges. States allow between 90 days and a year. These time periods are considerably shorter than those granted to most victims of battery, slander, negligence, and breach of contract. No justification exists for such a short statute of limitations, especially since it often takes harassment victims a long time to sort through their experience and decide on a course of action.

- *Apply the "reasonable woman" standard throughout the country.* In 1991, the Ninth Circuit Court recognized that some workplace actions considered harmless by men can be threatening to women. Technically, this ruling holds only within the geographic area where it originated (on the West Coast). The "reasonable woman" standard should have the force of law throughout the nation, on both the state and federal level.

- *Remove the limit on damage awards.* The Civil Rights Act of 1991 took a big step forward by allowing harassment victims to collect compensatory and punitive damages for the first time. But by imposing a limit on how much money the victim can collect, the Act sends a message that sex discrimination is not as serious as other kinds of legal violations.

  Some fear that allowing unlimited damages will result in an avalanche of gigantic awards. In fact, in states where unlimited damages are permitted—such as Alaska, California, New Jersey, and New York—large awards are rare. Nonetheless, the threat of a large award can help motivate employers to prevent harassment. The federal government and all states should allow unlimited damage awards.

- *Allow state fair-employment agencies to sue.* Federal law on harassment applies only to firms with 15 or more employees. To protect workers in small firms, fair-employment agencies in every state should have the power not only to mediate between victim and employer, but to go to court as well.

- *Improve unemployment compensation statutes.* Harassment victims who quit their jobs and apply for unemployment benefits face an uncertain fate. In some states, they receive benefits; in others, they're turned down because they are deemed to have left their jobs "voluntarily." In *every* state, quitting a job because of sexual harassment should be defined as a "constructive discharge"—the equivalent of an involuntary dismissal without cause—and the victim should be entitled to compensation.

- *Train judges, lawyers, and agency staff.* Personnel at all levels of the legal-enforcement system need to be educated about harassment if victims are to receive competent representation and a fair hearing. Some states have appointed task forces to study sex bias in their judicial systems. Such reviews should be conducted nationwide.

Is a work world free of harassment in the future? It can be, provided that the necessary steps are taken to create it.

Appendix A

Resource List

9to5, National Association of Working Women
614 Superior Ave. NW
Cleveland, OH 44113-1387
Toll-free Job Problem Hotline: **1-800-522-0925**
  (in Cleveland, **621-9449**)

Business and Professional Women/USA
2012 Massachusetts Ave. NW
Washington, DC 20036
(202) 293-1100

Coalition of Labor Union Women
15 Union Square
New York, NY 10003
(212) 242-0700 (information on unions and union policies)

District 925
1313 L Street NW
Washington, DC 20005
(202) 898-3200

Equal Employment Opportunity Commission
1-800-669-EEOC

Equal Rights Advocates
1663 Mission Street, Suite 550
San Francisco, CA 94103
(415) 621-0505 (legal counseling and advice in Spanish and
  English)

Federally Employed Women
1400 Eye Street NW
Washington, DC 20005
(202) 898-0994

National Council on Research for Women
The Sara Delano Roosevelt Memorial House
47-49 East 65th Street
New York, NY 10021
(212) 570-5001

NOW Legal Defense & Education Fund
99 Hudson Street
New York, NY 10013 (detailed model policy and legal
    resource kit)

Wider Opportunities for Women, Inc.
1325 G Street NW (LL)
Washington, DC 20005
(202) 638-3143 (network of local advocacy centers)

Appendix B

Offices of the Equal Employment Opportunity Commission

GENERAL INFORMATION

1-800-669-EEOC
(202) 634-7057 for the hearing impaired

DISTRICT OFFICES

Albuquerque, NM: (505) 766-2061
Atlanta, GA: (404) 331-6093
Baltimore, MD: (301) 962-3932
Birmingham, AL: (205) 731-0082
Boston, MA: (617) 565-3200
Buffalo, NY: (716) 846-4441
Charlotte, NC: (704) 567-7100
Chicago, IL: (312) 353-2713
Cincinnati, OH: (513) 684-2851
Cleveland, OH: (216) 522-2001
Dallas, TX: (214) 767-7015
Denver, CO: (303) 866-1300
Detroit, MI: (313) 226-7636
El Paso, TX: (915) 534-6550
Fresno, CA: (209) 487-5793
Greensboro, NC: (919) 333-5174

Greenville, SC: (803) 241-4400
Honolulu, HI: (808) 541-3120
Houston, TX: (713) 653-3320
Indianapolis, IN: (317) 226-7212
Jackson, MS: (601) 965-4537
Kansas City, MO: (816) 426-5773
Little Rock, AR: (501) 324-5060
Los Angeles, CA: (213) 251-7278
Louisville, KY: (502) 582-6082
Memphis, TN: (901) 722-2617
Miami, FL: (305) 536-4491
Milwaukee, WI: (414) 297-1111
Minneapolis, MN: (612) 370-3330
Nashville, TN: (615) 736-5820
Newark, NJ: (201) 645-6383
New Orleans, LA: (504) 589-2329
New York, NY: (212) 264-7161
Norfolk, VA: (804) 441-3470
Oakland, CA: (510) 273-7588
Oklahoma City, OK: (405) 231-4911
Philadelphia, PA: (215) 656-7020
Phoenix, AZ: (602) 640-5000
Pittsburgh, PA: (412) 644-3444
Raleigh, NC: (919) 856-4064
Richmond, VA: (804) 771-2692
San Antonio, TX: (512) 229-4810
San Diego, CA: (619) 557-7235
San Francisco, CA: (415) 744-6500
San Jose, CA: (408) 291-7352
Savannah, GA: (912) 944-4234
Seattle, WA: (206) 553-0968
St. Louis, MO: (314) 425-6585
Tampa, FL: (813) 228-2310
Washington, DC: (202) 275-7377

Appendix C

Equal Employment Opportunity Commission's Charge of Discrimination Form

This form is affected by the Privacy Act of 1974; See Privacy Act Statement before completing this form.

CHARGE OF DISCRIMINATION

AGENCY	CHARGE NUMBER
☐ FEPA	
☒ EEOC	

State or local Agency, if any ———————— and EEOC

NAME (Indicate Mr., Ms., Mrs.)	HOME TELEPHONE (Include Area Code)

STREET ADDRESS	CITY, STATE AND ZIP CODE	DATE OF BIRTH / /

NAMED IS THE EMPLOYER, LABOR ORGANIZATION, EMPLOYMENT AGENCY APPRENTICESHIP COMMITTEE, STATE OR LOCAL GOVERNMENT AGENCY WHO DISCRIMINATED AGAINST ME (If more than one list below.)

NAME	NUMBER OF EMPLOYEES, MEMBERS	TELEPHONE (Include Area Code)

STREET ADDRESS	CITY, STATE AND ZIP CODE	COUNTY

NAME	TELEPHONE NUMBER (Include Area Code)

STREET ADDRESS	CITY, STATE AND ZIP CODE	COUNTY

CAUSE OF DISCRIMINATION BASED ON (Check appropriate box(es))

☐ RACE ☐ COLOR ☐ SEX ☐ RELIGION ☐ NATIONAL ORIGIN
☐ RETALIATION ☐ AGE ☐ DISABILITY ☐ OTHER (Specify)

DATE DISCRIMINATION TOOK PLACE
EARLIEST (ADEA/EPA) / / LATEST (ALL) / /
☐ CONTINUING ACTION

THE PARTICULARS ARE (If additional space is needed, attach extra sheet(s)):

☐ I also want this charge filed with the EEOC. I will advise the agencies if I change my address or telephone number and I will cooperate fully with them in the processing of my charge in accordance with their procedures.

I declare under penalty of perjury that the foregoing is true and correct.

Date	Charging Party (Signature)

NOTARY - (When necessary for State and Local Requirements)

I swear or affirm that I have read the above charge and that it is true to the best of my knowledge, information and belief.

SIGNATURE OF COMPLAINANT

SUBSCRIBED AND SWORN TO BEFORE ME THIS DATE (Day, month, and year)

EEOC TEST FORM 5 (09/01/91)

FILE COPY

149

Appendix D

Examples of Antidiscrimination Clauses for Union Contracts

"Every employee has the right to equal treatment by the company with respect to all aspects of the exercise of managerial authority by the company, which equal treatment shall be without discrimination because of race, ancestry, place of origin, color, ethnic origin, citizenship, creed, religion, political affiliation, sex, record of criminal offenses, age, marital status, family status, handicap, sexual preference, and membership or office in the union." (**United Steelworkers of America, Canada**)

"The employer agrees that there shall be no interference, restriction, or coercion exercised or practiced with respect to any employee in the matter of hiring, wage rates, training, upgrading, promotion, transfer, lay-off, recall, discipline, classification, discharge, or otherwise by reason of age, race, creed, color, national origin, political or religious affiliation, sex or marital status, sexual orientation, place of residence, family relationship, nor by reason of his or her membership in the union." (**Service Employees International Union**)

"The employer and the union agree to cooperate in a policy of equal opportunity for all employees. Discrimination because of race, color, sex, religion, age or union activity is expressly prohibited." (**American Federation of State, County, & Municipal Employees**)

"If you have any questions about what constitutes discriminating behavior, ask the Personnel Department." (**United Railroad Workers**)

ABOUT 9TO5

If you're having any kind of problem on the job—sexual harassment, concerns about pregnancy or maternity leave, discrimination in pay or benefits, health and safety—call the 9to5 Job Problem Hotline. Our trained counselors can give you the advice and support you need.

9to5 JOB PROBLEM HOTLINE
1-800-522-0925

— —

9to5, National Association of Working Women, would welcome you as a member. Complete this form and mail it to:

> 9to5, National Association of Working Women
> 614 Superior Avenue, NW
> Cleveland, OH 44113

————— I would like to join 9to5. Enclosed please find my check for $25 made out to 9to5.

————— Enclosed is my tax-deductible contribution to 9to5, Working Women Education Fund, the research and education arm of 9to5.

————— I will designate my payroll deduction to 9to5, Working Women Education Fund. Please send me a reminder.

Charge my dues/contribution to my:

————— Visa ————— Mastercard Expiration Date _____

Credit Card # _____ Signature _____

————— My dues are enclosed. Please send me information on starting a 9to5 chapter or becoming a local 9to5 representative.

————— Please send me more information on 9to5.

Name _____

Address _____

City/State _____

Phone (home) _____ (work) _____

Job title _____ Industry _____